U0084664

How to Write
a Successful Resume

陳瓊芳 修編　　Bruce S. Stewart 校閱

LEARNING PUBLISHING CO., LTD.

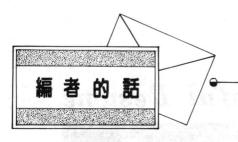

編者的話

這是一個自我推銷的時代。

不管您是即將踏入社會，或是正考慮換個新工作，都需要將自己的能力及優秀的一面呈現給雇主；而履歷表正扮演著這個穿針引線又舉足輕重的地位。科技縮短了時空的距離，外語能力便成了一項不容忽視的資格條件，因此寫出一份簡潔、明確、漂亮的英文履歷表，才能適切地達到自我推銷的目的。

「如何寫好英文履歷表」即在引導讀者掌握先機，爭取應徵過程中第一回合的勝利，以獲得面試的機會。第一篇**英文履歷表入門**先就履歷表作說明，並告訴您怎麼樣的長度、用語、語氣才能構成一篇成功的英文履歷表。第二篇**英文履歷表的黃金組合**剖析了履歷表的構成要素，並且該如何利用這些要素，生動而有吸引力的表達出自己的適任資格及能力。

第三篇**英文履歷表的寫作技巧**除了告訴讀者如何編列漂亮的格式，並搜集了實用的詞彙及佳句，以供參考應用。第四篇**英文履歷表範例**共有二十六篇範文，不僅格式編排經過精心設計，內容更因應文法工商各行各業的需要，適合正欲求職或正在謀職的您採納參考。

附函（*Cover Letter*）和履歷表有相得益彰之趣，附上附函不僅是禮貌的表示，內容上更可補充履歷表中未能詳盡之處。我們編入了第五篇**英文履歷表的最佳拍檔──附函**，針對其功用形式作一目瞭然的解說，並列出書寫附函時的重點。

第六篇**附函範例**是配合第四篇履歷表的範文所寫，二十六篇信函篇篇精彩豐富，就應屆畢業或已有工作經驗，看報應徵或自我推薦等各個狀況，作不同方式的表達。

只要您詳細閱讀，並且參考各章節的範例及範文，相信將使您胸有成竹，寫出一份成功的英文履歷表和附函，達到推銷自我的目的，讓雇主對您留下深刻的印象，而在眾多的應試者中脫穎而出。

追求盡善盡美是我們一貫的目標與原則。本書雖經多次審慎的校對，仍恐有疏漏之處，尚祈各界先進不吝惠予指教。

CONTENTS

第一篇

英文履歷表入　　門

1. 什麼是英文履歷表

2. 成功的英文履歷表要訣

How to Write a Successful Resume

1.什麼是英文履歷表

　　Resume 在這裏是指新式的英文履歷表。以前稱爲 personal history（個人歷史）或 curriculum vitae（履歷）。現在一般在美國則通用 resume 這個字。偶而也有 data sheet 或 vita，vitae 的用法。在美國的圖書出版目錄裏，可以發現關於 resume 的書籍有六十本以上。其他在 Business communication 類的書中，也都有特別說明。

　　Resume 並不是將經驗一一列舉，而是列出主要的且相關的經驗、業績、能力、性格等等，將它們**簡潔有力**的整理出來，就像自己是個 sales person（salesman or saleswoman），利用 resume 來推銷自己，是就業中不可缺少的文件。它能夠引起雇主對你的關心，所以不要光寫過去，必須明瞭有效地把未來的發展以重點式的書面報告表達出來。

　　在寫履歷表時，往往要分析評估自己，這可以幫助自己明確了解未來的方向，即使未想就業時，也可先學習如何展現己長。

　　由於它是就業的第一關，必須使它出色；吸引人的題材是必然的條件，務使它簡潔且不失重點。一般而言，英文履歷表並沒有固定的格式，可隨個人喜好定出格式，但是仍要注意掌握下列要點：

　　① 積極表現自己的優點

　　② 對雇主而言重要的資料要先寫出來

　　③ 具體地寫出業績和成果

　　④ 不要寫一般平常的資料，要寫出特出的

　　⑤ 注意統一性和均衡性

英文履歷表的用途

英文履歷表可在下列情況下派上用場：

① 看到報上登有求才廣告時，可以寄出去。

② 即使沒有徵才廣告時，也可以寄到想去服務的公司。

③ 訪問招募人員的公司時，可以帶幾份去。

④ 拜託朋友幫忙找工作時，可以交給他們。

⑤ 和學校指導教官、就業輔導人員、及親戚朋友商量就業時，可以當作資料。

⑥ 面試時，可以作爲談論自己的基礎資料。

⑦ 面試之後，要留幾份給雇主存檔用，或給有關人員傳閱用。

⑧ 填寫雇主的申請表（Application Form）時，可作參考。

由於申請書因各公司而有差異，但項目大致和英文履歷表相似，所以隨身攜帶會很方便。

【 Conclusion 】：

履歷表是針對自己想應徵的工作，把所備的資格經歷簡要地列舉出來，以達到推銷自己的目的，獲得面試的機會，增加錄取的機率。它可以把你直接推銷給雇主，對爭取面試而言，是一個相當重要的關鍵文件。由於它是屬於目錄形式的，就必須整理得簡潔有序，使雇主能夠眼睛一亮，對你留下深刻的印象，萬萬不可失於繁瑣冗雜。

How to Write a Successful Resume

2. 成功的英文履歷表要訣

對英文履歷表一個基本的概念就是，要讓雇主在**很短的時間中**能瞭解，你能為他作什麼，所以必須簡潔、有個性、有魅力地敍述自己。

 ## 站在雇主的立場來考慮

寫商業書信時的一個基本要件，就是 *You-attitude*，也就是要我們站在讀者的立場來考慮。同樣地，在寫英文履歷表時，應用 You-Attitude，就讓它變得簡潔、明瞭，而且具體。

考慮到雇主的立場，首先要寫出他想知道的內容，告訴他就業之後，能為公司貢獻什麼；你的課外活動及工讀等資料都可以作為判斷你能力時的參考。在字裏行間，一定要依照事實，不要誇張，並且寫出你的性向及適應能力。

 ## 如何避免失敗的英文履歷表

要寫出一份成功的履歷表，必須注意避免下列情況發生：

① 版面設計不好的履歷表。（這會導致第一印象不好。）

② 應徵項目不明，讓雇主難以判斷你所希望的職務是什麼。

③ 沒有寫明具備的資格。

④ 沒寫明過去的職稱及負責的工作。

⑤ 沒寫以前的工作成績。

⑥ 經歷不完整 。（ 令人懷疑沒有工作時 ，究竟在作什麼 。）

⑦ 漏了重要數字 。（ 這會降低這份文件的可信度 。）

⑧ 太冗長的說明 ，錯別字或文法錯誤 。（ 令人懷疑你的辦事能力 。）

吸引人的英文履歷表

英文履歷表最主要就是要**爭取到面試的機會**，所以必須儘量表現出自己的優點 ，表示自己適合於這份工作 ，因此可以由那份工作的角度來分析自己的經歷、學歷或者資格及技能 。

英文履歷表的寫法相當自由 ，並無固定的格式 ，因此優劣差異非常的大 。在選擇題材內容時 ，經歷少的年輕人應先寫學歷再寫經歷 ，而工作經驗豐富的人 ，可以考慮先寫工作經歷 ，而且按照時間或工作性質來排列 。

長度適宜

在長度方面 ，也沒有一定的標準 ，但仍以**一至二頁**爲佳 。和工作有關以及雇主關心的資料 ，可以寫在前面 ，如果資料太多 ，則用大張紙寫後再縮小 。

用語妥切

閱讀的前幾秒便已決定了第一印象 ，於是遣詞用字方面必須謹慎 ，而且負責的人必定是很忙的 ，因此簡潔有力的字是必然的 。

必須特別留意的一點是**"I"的省略**。提了太多次 ，不僅令人煩厭 ，又有自傲之感 ，並且缺乏效率 。

例如：

I reorganized marketing strategies of...

我重編…的市場戰略。

最好改成：

Reorganized marketing strategies of...

重編的…市場戰略。

把 " I " 省略。

動詞意味的用語，生動活潑，應當善加利用。這在本書第三篇中列有常用字彙，讀者可參考使用。

至於一般的簡稱，如Bachelor of Arts 可簡稱BA外，儘量少用簡稱，以避免損及英文履歷表的優雅。而專用術語，除非肯定負責人能了解，否則少用為妙。

【 Summary 】：

關於英文履歷表一個很基本的概念就是，務必使雇主在很短的時間之內，便能瞭解你具備了什麼樣的資格，以及你能為他作些什麼。因此一份履歷表必須兼備有魅力、有個性、又簡潔扼要的特色，才能有效地傳達你的資格與目的給雇主。

至於英文履歷表的形式並不一定，必須選擇最適合自己的內容及格式，並且配合謀求的職務，作一最佳的搭配。

第二篇

英文履歷表的
黃金組合

Personal Data
個人資料

個人資料包括籍貫、婚姻、子女、性別、身高、體重、照片等。寫的時候可以列成如表狀：

《個人資料》

Permanent Domicile	:	Taipei
Marital Status	:	Married (*or* Single)
Children	:	3 children (*or* none, etc.)
Sex	:	Male (*or* Female)
Hight	:	5′－4″ (*or* 162 cm)
Weight	:	120 lbs (*or* 55 kg)

籍　貫	:	台北
婚姻狀況	:	已婚（或未婚）
子　女	:	3個（或無，等等）
性　別	:	男（或女）
身　高	:	5呎4吋（或162公分）
體　重	:	120磅（或55公斤）

性別除了上面的寫法外，也可以就在名字前面附上 Mr.、Miss.、Mrs.（或以 Ms. 代替 Miss 與 Mrs）。

姓名因為沒有一定的格式，所以千萬別漏了寫，以免雇主聯絡不到你。可以在每一頁的開頭寫上姓名、頁數，以方便雇主閱讀。如下：

Chung- chieh Lee　　　　　　　　　　　　　　　*Page 2*

　　另外還有一些增加效果的資料：比如說外語能力、海外經歷、傳眞機和電腦的操作能力等。

Language：German — Fluent in reading and speaking
　　　　　　Spanish — Conversational

外　語：德文——說、讀流利
　　　　西班牙文——會話程度

　　國外生活、長期海外旅行，會使你對各國的人民及文化有某種程度的了解，並且也可以證明你的外語能力。如果曾長住於和業務關係密切的國家，那麼對你的**資格**也會大有助益。例如：

Traveled extensively throughout North America while staying in N.Y. for three years accompanying parents.

陪父母留住紐約三年期間，廣遊北美各地。

Lived in New York twice while father was stationed there as a member of a major trading company. First four years before school age and second four years as senior high school student.

當父親是一家大貿易公司一員時，派駐紐約，曾經兩度住在紐約。最初四年是學齡前，後來四年是高中時代。

　　如果會操作傳眞機、電腦等，要寫出純熟度。

例：Typing	50wpm	Computer Language	Cobol
打　字	一分鐘50字	電腦語言	Cobol

　　至於照片，在美國除了特別須要求容貌的行業之外，法律是禁止要求照片的，而在我國則不然，把照片附在信封內可以加强雇主對您的印象。

如果健康情形非常好，當然要特別强調或從運動項目裏也可以間接表示您的健康情形。

Excellent health ································· 健康極佳

如果是需要出差、調職的工作，最好先表示自己願意接受這種變動。因爲可能有很多人因有家室之累，不願意去外地上班。

Willing to travel································· 願意出差

Willing to relocate······························· 願意調遷

【Example】：以下是一個說明自己外語能力的個人資料寫法。

Su-huey Yang
Born: November 22, 1986
Dual Citizenship: Chinese and Japanese
Languages: fluent Mandarin, Japanese, and English
　　　　　I was born in Japan. My mother is Japanese and my father is Chinese. My family returned to Taiwan when I was 12 and I was enrolled in a local high school here. After high school I attended the Chinese Cultural University, majoring in English. I am thus trilingual, being fluent in Mandarin, Japanese and English.

楊淑慧
生日：1986 年 11 月 22 日
雙重國籍：中國和日本
語言：中文、日文、英文流利
　　　　我出生於日本，我的母親是日本人，而父親是中國人。十二歲時，全家回到台灣，我就讀於當地的中學。中學之後，我就讀於中國文化大學，主修英文。因此我可以說三種語言，中文、日文、英文都流利。

Job Objective/Qualifications
希望的職務和自己的資格

在英文履歷表一開頭的位置，具體而扼要地寫出你所**希望的職務**（Job objective），直接表示出你的目的和動機，可以給人一個好印象。

體裁是予人好印象的要件。就像一幅畫必須要有焦點，以吸引雇主的眼睛。它使履歷表看來有統一性。

最好把 resume 的焦點都集中在你未來的目標上。也就是將來預期的最高職務上，如此，對雇主來說，可以很快了解你的目標。例：

* Objective ……………………………… 希望職務
* Position wanted ……………………… 希望職位

或者更直接寫出：

* Executive secretary ………………… 業務祕書
* Sales manager ………………………… 行銷部經理
* Chief accountant ……………………… 會計主任
* Systems analyst ……………………… 系統分析師
* Programmer …………………………… 程式設計師

不要寫得很籠統，要儘量具體。如果將下例更改一下會更好：

* Personnel work ……………………… 人事工作

改成：

* Personnel recruitment ……………… 人事招募

但是有些雇主喜歡比較有彈性、靈活的說法。

* Acceptance in a management training program
  接受管理訓練計畫
* Entry-level position in an accounting environment
  會計部門的初級職位
* Responsible entry position in computer programming
  員責電腦程式設計的初級職位

這些比較客氣的表達方式，通常適用於剛踏入社會的工作者。

還有一種情況，就是把將來希望升遷的職位寫出來。在美國，他們希望求職者能夠把他心中的意欲清楚地寫出來，包括目前的希望，以及將來想達到的職位。不過，這在我國不是很普遍，不如面談時再說比較好。如果雇主要求你敘述將來希望的職位時，不妨這樣寫：

* Career Objective ···································· 事業目標
* Clerical position to start. Career objective is an
  accounting position.
    從書記職位開始。事業目標是一份會計的職位。
* Entry-level marketing-trainee position with opportunities
  for advancement.
    有進昇機會的初級市場見習生職位。

◆　　　　　◆　　　　　◆

* A sales representative position. Eventual goal is to
  become a manager in the marketing department.
    銷售代表的職位。最終目標是成為銷售部門的經理。
* Entry-level position in Accounting. Long-range goal
  Financial Management.
    會計的初級職位。長期目標是財經管理工作。

寫清楚希望的職務後，必須將你的資格（Qualifications）寫清楚，讓雇主了解你的經驗、性向、能力。

　　我們可以從求才廣告上得知雇主所要求的資格，或是朋友、公司簡介中得到消息。如下例：

1　Management trainees in Marketing Department. University graduates, preferably business administration major with emphasis in marketing.

　　在市場部門接受管理訓練的人員。大學畢業，以市場銷售為重，主修企業管理尤佳。

由這則廣告中，我們可以知道雇主的要求：

　① 徵求將來希望能晉升到管理階層的人士

　② 不注重經歷

　③ 大學畢，主修企管或市場學

　　　　　　✦　　　　　　✦　　　　　　✦

2　Executive assistant to the controller. Secretarial skills, broad background in accounting essential. Extensive writing.

　　高級主管的執行助理。須備祕書技能且對基本會計常識有廣泛經歷。能勝任大量文書作業。

由此可知其要求：

　① 主管的助理

　② 擁有祕書及處理經理業務經驗的人

　③ 能夠有效處理大量商業書信的人

　　想換工作時，如果和你現在、及過去有的工作經驗性質相似的話，就可以根據經歷來強調你所具備的資格。如果想應徵的工作，與過去的不相似，也要盡量找出它們的共通點才行。

　　如果都沒有共通點的話，那就要強調您的學歷和個性了。如果您是尚未畢業的學生，都沒有社會經驗，或者才剛踏入社會，經歷較少，這時您可以把和業務有關的專業科目及學業成績，再加上工讀的經驗統統寫上去。理由如下：

① 你的主修科目和所應徵的工作有關，這當然是雇主所希望的，成績好表示你的智力高，外商投資的公司特別欣賞。雖然有外商公司沒有那麼重視學業成績，但成績優秀畢竟還是比較有利。

② 賺學費來打工，可以顯示你的意志力很強，即使你工讀的內容和應徵的工作沒有直接的關係，但你的態度、勤奮、協調性、對人關係等經驗，都是很好的資料。尊重個性的外商公司，非常重視協調性，這一點我們可以在很多的求人廣告中看到。

若履歷表的內容太少，那麼也可以把個性中和工作有關的特徵寫上去，如領導能力、機智、人際外交、沈著細心、果決，如此更可以加添履歷表的人情味，而且更生動。

在寫資格這個項目時，得簡單扼要。因為在後面的學歷、經歷中還會提到，所以只是要先寫個**重點**，以吸引雇主讀下去，達到良好之效。如下：

Bacheler of Arts in Business Administration...major in marketing. Two years of summer-job experience working with fine chemicals marketing people.

企業管理學士…主修市場銷售。有與精密化學品製造銷售人員共事兩年的暑期工作經驗。

這資格也可以寫在附函裏，不須在履歷表上另設項目。完全依履歷表的內容而定，不是絕對的。

Work Experience
工作經歷

　　如果有很多經歷，在應徵時，想特別強調這一點時，就把經歷寫在學歷之前。公司名稱、服務期間都要寫清楚，負責的工作及工作績效也要具體地記載，頭銜表示你的職責，對完成工作的程度非常重要，和業務有關的進修也可以列出來，如果沒有困難，也可以寫出調職的理由。

 ## 經歷書寫的順序

　　一般來說，目前的工作可以說是最重要的工作。因此，就從目前的工作開始寫起，而且要寫得最詳細，強調你認為最重要的資料。如果以前的工作和你想應徵的工作，關係較密切的話，就先寫那份工作經歷，而且要寫得最詳細。

 ## 公司名稱和地址

　　要把以前服務的公司名稱及簡單的地址寫下來。如果你認為應徵負責人對你以前的服務公司不太了解的話，可以在括弧內簡單地敍述公司的內容。如果不想讓目前的服務公司知道你正在應徵其他工作的話，就不要寫公司名稱。

* A Leading Electronics Maker
  主要的電子產品製造商

* A Major Trading Company
  一家大型貿易公司

服務期間

　　必須要把在各個公司的服務期間，從第一天上班到離職為止的日期寫出來，寫法有很多種。可以把日期寫在公司名稱的左邊，如下：

* April 2003 to March 2008　　Pacific Trading Co., Ltd.
　2003年4月至2008年3月　　太平洋貿易有限公司

在各個公司服務時的頭銜，要寫在日期之後，例如：

* 4/06－3/08 Assistant Manager, Overseas Sales Dep't
　4/03－3/06 Manager, North America Section, Overseas
　　Sales Dep't
　2006年4月－2008年3月　　海外行銷部門助理經理
　2003年4月－2006年3月　　海外行銷部門，北美分部經理

也可以把公司名稱寫在前面，把服務日期寫在後面。

* Instructor, Department of Sociology, Taiwan University
　（June 2005 － May 2007）
　台灣大學社會學系講師（ 2005年6月至2007年5月 ）

　　但是，你目前是不是還在工作，這對雇主來說是一項很重要的資料。因此，如果你目前還在工作，就要用下面的寫法。

* April 2000 to Present ‧‧‧‧‧‧‧‧‧‧‧‧‧‧‧‧‧‧‧‧‧‧‧‧‧‧‧‧‧‧‧ 2000年4月至今

如果你目前已不在那家公司了，就要把離職的日期寫清楚。

* April 2000 to December 2007 ‧‧‧‧‧‧‧ 2000年4月至2007年12月

如果你寫這樣

* April 2000 to － ‧‧‧‧‧‧‧‧‧‧‧‧‧‧‧‧‧‧‧‧‧‧‧‧‧‧‧‧‧‧‧ 2000 年4月至‧‧‧

那雇主根本不知道你究竟還有沒有在工作，所以這一點一定要寫清楚。

負責的業務及業績

要**簡單扼要**地寫出你在每家公司所負責的業務以及業績。

▷ **職責**

具體地敍述你所擔任職務的責任,如下例:

1 Secretary to Marketing Manager.
   Responsibilities : Writing letters and reports, doing research, planning conferences and meetings.
   市場銷售經理祕書
   職責:書寫信件和報告,調查,計劃討論會及會議。

　　　　　　＊　　　　　　　＊　　　　　　　＊

2 Secretary to Purchasing Manager.
   Responsibilities : General secretarial activities, such as receiving visitors, making appointments, taking dictation, writing routine letters.
   採購部經理祕書
   職責:一般祕書業務,例如接見訪客,安排約會,記錄口述,書寫例行信件。

　　　　　　＊　　　　　　　＊　　　　　　　＊

3 Computer operator :
   Processed scheduled jobs, checked validity of output, distributed printouts, maintained list of utilization.
   電腦操作員
   處理排定的工作,檢查輸出的有效性,印表分類,維持目錄的利用。

④ Assistant to Manager of Accounting Department.
Responsible for accounts payable section: duties include
figuring discounts on statements of accounts, posting
accounts, writing checks.

會計部門經理助理
負責應付帳款部分：責任包括計算帳目報告書的折扣額，過帳，
書寫支票。

▷ 頭銜

通常，寫頭銜比寫職務內容更可以簡要地表示你所負責的職務。但
是光寫頭銜，對你的工作內容依然不是很清楚，要把具體的工作內容簡
單地說明，所以頭銜與職務二項都寫才妥當。

如果經歷很多的話，最近一次以外的工作只要寫頭銜就好。應徵的
負責人所關心的是你的適合性及最近幾年的經驗，以前你有些什麼經歷，
這只是給他做個參考而已。所以對於太久的事情只要略述即可。

* responsibilities include ·························· 職責包括
* responsible for······························· 負責…

負責的業務寫成 duties 的話，讓人有一種義務的、被動的感覺。如
果寫成 responsibilities，會使人覺得這不是單純的日常業務或固定的工
作，而是一種需要分析、評價、決斷及解決問題的職責，可以顯示出你
的工作的重要性。

至於強調的重點，可以放在和應徵工作有關的經驗上，如果沒有守
密義務，具體的顧客名稱和商品名稱，也很具效果。你的業績，像是降
低成本，增加銷售量，都可加以強調。如下例：

① District Sales Manager. Responsibilities: Training and su-
pervising a staff of 20. Territory includes all Taipei area.
Sales in the territory increased by 30% in 2008.

地區行銷經理。職責：訓練督導二十名職員，範圍包括整個台北地區。2008年此區域的銷售增加 30％。

　　　　＊　　　　　　　＊　　　　　　　＊

2　Programmer. Assisted in redesign of office information system resulting in 20％ reduction in costs.
程式設計師。
幫助公司資訊系統的再設計，達成降低 20％的成本。

只是，如果要寫數字的話，因為關係到各公司的秘密，所以要特別注意。這個時候，在履歷表上不要寫上數字，可用**百分比**來間接表示即可。

如果你完成了一些特別交待的事，那就一定要把它們寫出來，這表示你的能力和適應性受到上司肯定，這些是判斷你未來發展性的一個很好的資料。

3　Reduced cost by 50％ through new design, improved coordination of assembly line, transfer of key personnel to problem area.
藉新設計降低百分之五十的成本，改善裝配線的協調，調動機要人員到有問題的區域。

 上司的頭銜

把直屬上司的頭銜寫出來，也可明確地表示出你的職責及在公司內的地位。

＊ Secretary to the Vice President in charge of Foreign Exchange Operation.
負責外滙兌換作業之副總經理的祕書。

* Assistant to Marketing Manager
  市場銷售經理助理
* Assistant to Manager responsible for recruitment and training
  負責招募及訓練的經理助理

可以上班的時間

還在工作的話，可以在個人資料項目裏，或其他適當的地方，把什麼時候可以到新公司上班的時間寫清楚。

* Available July 1, 2009 ·············· 2009年7月1日就可以上班

換工作的理由

如果沒有困難的話，可以把換工作的理由寫出，給雇主知道。假使不寫在履歷表上，也可寫在附函裏面。

理由可能是企業合併，或希望增加工作的挑戰性，不管是那種理由，一定要清楚明白。

* due to close-down of plant ··············· 由於工廠關閉
* to seek a better job ························ 找一份較好的工作
* to look for a more challenging opportunity
  找一個更有挑戰性的工作機會
* sought a better job·························· 找份更好的工作
* offered a more challenging opportunity
  提供更有挑戰性的工作機會

如果你目前還在上班，換新工作的理由可以表示如下：

* for wider experience ····················· 為擴大工作經驗
* for higher responsibility ················· 為高層次的工作責任

* for more specialized work .... 為更專門的工作
* for prospects of promotion .... 為升遷的可能性

　　如果不能夠講清楚的話，只要寫上 "personal reason" 也可以，等面試時再加以說明。有一點一定要注意的是，千萬不要**批評**過去或現在的雇主。

 # 特別進修

　　如果你有過什麼樣的進修，那也要把在進修中所得到的經驗寫在履歷表上。包括公司內外的進修及國內外的留學等。

　　如果你覺得這些進修和你目前想應徵的工作關係密切的話，可以另外設個*Special Training*，和經歷分開寫。

> June 2008 to September 2008, Summer school in UCSD.
> Coursework includes: essays writing, introduction to
> business communication, public speaking, business
> English.

　　2008年6月至2008年9月，加州大學聖地牙哥分校暑期學校。
課程包括：論說文寫作，商務溝通概論，公眾演說，商用英文。

 # 其它經驗

　　當你擁有很多經歷時，有一種寫法，就是把經歷裏和應徵的工作有特別關係的，集中寫在*Work Experience*項下，其他的經歷則寫在*Other Experience*項裏。

Education 學 歷

　　因為還是學生，所以沒有社會經驗；或是才剛畢業沒多久，社會經歷較少；還是雖然有經歷，但是你認為對想應徵的工作來說，你的學歷比經歷重要。這個時候，就把學歷寫在最前面。

　　雖然學歷和業務沒有關連，但雇主可以經由學歷，去了解應徵者的智力、思考力、判斷力和個性。

 ## 書寫學歷的順序

　　寫學歷的順序，是從最近的開始寫，一直往前推移，寫法如下例：

《 學歷㈠ 》

Master of Science with concentration in Electronics
Massachusetts Institute of Technology（9/05－6/07）
Bachelor of Science
Taiwan University, Department of Electrical Engineer
（9/01－6/05）

麻省理工學院工學碩士,主修電子學（2005年9月－2007年6月）
台灣大學電機系學士（2001年9月－2005年6月）

《 學歷㈡ 》

September 2001－June 2005　　Chengchi University, Bachelor
　　　　　　　　　　　　　　　of Arts.　Department of In-
　　　　　　　　　　　　　　　ternational Business
September 1998－June 2001　　Kaohsiung High School

2001年9月—2005年6月　政治大學國際貿易系學士
1998年9月—2001年6月　高雄中學

《學歷㈢》

September 2004—June 2007　Chengchi University, Bachelor of Arts. Department of International Relations

September 2001—June 2004　The First High School, Taichung

2004年9月—2007年6月　政治大學國際關係系學士
2001年9月—2004年6月　台中一中

 # 修業科目

　　把在研究所和大學裏的專業科目中，和您所應徵的工作有密切關係的，具體地寫在學歷的項目下。

如：

《㈠》Major：International Management
　　　Minor：International Trade, Foreign Exchange

主修：國際管理
輔修：國際貿易，外滙兌換

《㈡》Major：Business Communication
　　　Minor：International Marketing, Cross-cultural Management.

主修：商務溝通
輔修：國際市場銷售，異文化管理學

　　把和應徵的工作有關連的科目**集中**起來，也是很有效果的。另外一種是把科目的內容，重點式地寫出。

《㈢》 Specialized courses contributing to management qualification:

　　　　Principles of Management, Theory of Business Administration, Organization Theory, Behavioral Science, Macroeconomics, Operations Research

　　助於管理資格的專門課程：

　　　　管理原理，商學管理論，組織學，行為科學，
　　　　總體經濟學，經營研究

✦　　　　　✦　　　　　✦

《㈣》 Courses taken that would be useful in secretarial work:

　　　　Secretarial Science, Office Management, Information Processing, Business English, Wordprocessing (in English), Bookkeeping, Filing

　　對祕書工作有用的課程：

　　　　祕書理論，辦公室管理，資料處理，商用英文，
　　　　英文文字處理，簿記，檔案處理

✦　　　　　✦　　　　　✦

《㈤》 Courses in Marketing and related field:

　　　　Marketing Principles, Sales Management, Distribution Theory, Economics, Accounting, Statistics, Psychology

　　市場銷售及相關領域的科目：

　　　　市場銷售原理，行銷管理，商品配銷論，經濟學，會計學，
　　　　統計學，心理學

✦　　　　　✦　　　　　✦

《㈥》 Special training in accounting:

　　　　Accounting Principles, Cost Accounting, Principles of Bookkeeping, Financial Management, EDP System

會計特別訓練：

　會計學原理，成本會計，簿記原理，財務管理，
　電子資料處理系統

 成　績

成績優越，獲得獎學金或是特別的成績，也可以列出來。

* A grade 120 out of total 130.
  總分130，成績120。
* Scholarship from President of the University
  大學校長獎學金
* President of Student Council
  學生會會長
* President of English Speaking Society
  英會社社長

【 **Key point** 】：要表示出曾修過那些和應徵工作相關的科目時，可以
有下列幾種說法——

　☆ Curriculum included:
　☆ Specialized courses contributing to personnel
　　 qualification:
　☆ Special training in secretarial work:
　☆ Courses in Management and related fields:
　☆ Courses taken that would be useful in programming:
　☆ Major: ～～～～～～～
　　 Minor: ～～～～～～～
　☆ Courses completed:
　☆ Courses taken include:

Summer Jobs/Part-time Jobs
工 讀

因為是學生，所以沒有經歷，或者剛畢業沒多久，經歷較少。這個時候，代替經歷的，就是暑期工讀或開學時的工讀了。它的寫法也是從最近的開始寫，然後向前推移。

工讀，並不僅僅把種類寫出來就好，還要包括在何處、擔任什麼工作、結果如何、從工讀中學到了什麼等。要把工讀當作經歷一樣，儘量寫詳細，表達出你的積極、負責、勤奮。

工讀的內容如果和您所應徵的工作沒有很密切的關係的話，處理的方式就不同了。如果關連性和內容都很少的話，倒不如不要寫的好。但是，即使關連性和內容都很少，而却從中**完成什麼**，或**得到什麼經驗**的話，都可以把它們寫下來，因為它可以顯示自己的意志、責任感、及能力，非常有意義。

總之，可以從工讀的重要性，來決定該如何處理履歷表。

《一》Summer 2006 and 2007, Waiter at The Grand Hotel：
In addition to routine waiter's responsibilities, served as assistant manager responsible for training waiters and waitresses.

2006 及 2007年暑假，在圓山大飯店當服務生：
除了日常服務生之職責外，充當助理經理，負責訓練男女服務生。

【**Key Point**】：訓練、監督人員，可以表示你的領導能力。

《二》September 2005 to June 2007, Worked part-time as office clerk for Sun Yang Co. Work involved typing, filing and preparing reports, proof-reading.

2005年9月至2007年6月，在三洋公司當兼差的事務職員。
工作包括打字，檔案處理和準備報告，校對。

【Key Point】：擔任報告書的準備及校對工作，可以顯示出處理事務的能力以及思考周密。

❀   ❀   ❀

《三》September 2006 to June 2007, Teaching Assistant at Tamkang University. Responsible for programming, checking system malfunctions, assisting students with computer jobs, keeping time-sharing records on all users.

2006年9月到2007年6月，擔任淡江大學助教。負責程式設計，檢查系統故障，輔導學生作電腦工作，管理所有使用者的時間分配記錄。

【Key Point】：擔任助教，負責多項工作，表示能力相當優越。

❀   ❀   ❀

《四》Summers 2006 and 2007, Part-timer at Sun Super Market. Managed inventory, established inventory re-order schedule, reported month-end sales reports. Gained products knowledge. Learned to work well with others.

2006年和2007年夏天在陽光超級市場兼差。
管理存貨。建立存貨重訂進度表。報告月底銷售。得到產品方面的知識。學習與他人好好工作。

【Key Point】：擔任倉庫管理，負責有系統的工作，利用這個機會，可以學到商品知識，培養人際關係。

Extracurricular Activities
課外活動

　　如果能夠參加多采多姿的課外活動，就表示你希望擴大自己的經驗，發揮多方面的才能，喜好與人交往，同時也可表示人格修養、成熟及健康狀態。例如曾經擔任學生會的會長，表示你擁有處理人際關係的能力，積極而且具領導能力。曾是辯論社的一員，表示自己可以在眾人面前表現得很穩重。

　　因此，如果曾經參加過什麼課外活動，就寫出來。這些事情可以顯示將來就業時，你的**適應性**，當雇主挑選人員的時候，會是項有利的條件。所以課外活動，對於仍在求學、尚無社會經歷的人來說，是應徵工作時的一個相當重要的要素。

1. Active in college student council.
   Senior year : President, organized campus festival.
   Junior year : Secretary, promoted foreign students club.
   活躍於大學學生會
   四年級：會長，組織校慶活動
   三年級：祕書，協辦外籍學生會

＊　　　　　　＊　　　　　　＊

2. President, Taiwan University ESS（English Speaking Society）
   Won All Taipei English Oratorical Contest, 2006.
   台灣大學英語社社長。　2006年全台北英語演說競賽優勝。

3 Captain, College Soccer Team.
Contributed to the winning of All Taiwan Soccer Contest.
大學足球隊隊長。
全台灣足球賽優勝貢獻。

社會活動

　　如果參加了一些社會性的活動，如擔任公司或學會的委員等，這正表示你的關心層面及與人的協調性，可能做為將來是否**晉升更高層次**的工作的參考。

　　如果你曾經擔任過負責人或幹部，就要把它寫清楚，但是，除了重要事項及年月外，其他的要省略。如果沒有什麼重要的內容，可以把社會活動挪到個人資料的項目。

1 July 2005 – June 2006, Membership Chairman, ABC Club:
Increased membership by 20%.
2005 年 7 月至 2006 年 6 月，ABC 社團委員長。
社團人數增加 20%。

＊　　　　　＊　　　　　＊

2 January 2007 to present, membership of Zonta Club:
Organized the Women's Day Festival.
2007 年 1 月至今，崇她社會員：
組織婦女節慶祝活動。

＊　　　　　＊　　　　　＊

3 April 2007 to November 2007, membership of Chinese Dramatic Arts Center, in charge of public relations.
2007 年 4 月至 2007 年 11 月，中國戲劇藝術中心會員，負責公共關係事務。

4 January 2005 to December 2007 . Secretary, Child Welfare
   Center .

   2005 年 1 月至 2007 年 12 月。
   兒童福利中心，祕書。

　　　　　　＊　　　　　　　＊　　　　　　　＊

5 Managing editor, Semi-Weekly of Tonyan Trading Co.,
   Ltd, November 2006 to April 2007 .
   東揚貿易股份有限公司半月刊總編輯 ， 2006年11月至2007年4月

 興　　趣

　　興趣可以說明**性格**及**成熟度**。若興趣可以加深雇主對你的印象，或
是和應徵工作有直接關係時，都可以列出來。但是要注意以下幾點：

(1) 寫出和他人一起享受的興趣，可以表現你的社交性。

(2) 只寫出有關係的興趣，否則予人花費太多時間和精力的印象。

(3) 如果沒有什麼興趣，不寫出來也無所謂，否則在面談提到興趣時，
　　說不起勁，反而有負面影響。

(4) 興趣必須寫清楚。

・Tennis （active, every Sunday）　Baseball （spectator —
　professional game）
　網球（每星期日打球）　　棒球（觀看職業棒賽）

Technical Qualifications/Special Skills /Publications/Patents
檢定資格・特殊技能・著作・專利權

檢定資格（ *Technical Qualifications* ）

　　檢定資格是一項重要的要素，表示你所擁有的技能，也表示你是個努力的人，所以應該書寫下來，最好也能準備好證明書。

+ Abacus Caculation 3rd class, 2007.
  2007 年，珠算三級。

+ Scored well on the National Ordinary Examination, 2008.
  2008 年，普考高分考過。

+ Passed the Examination for Promotion and Qualification, B grade, 2008.
  2008 年，升等檢定考試，乙等及格。

+ Received high marks on the Central Bank Special Examination, 2007.
  2007 年，中央銀行特考高分考過。

特殊技能（ *Special Skills* ）

　　如果對自己的特殊才能有信心的話，就要把它列舉出來。像是外國語文，特定的機器和電腦語言，都包括在其中。

+ Spanish: working knowledge（ conversational ）
  西班牙文：應用知識（會話方面）

+ Competency in writing and speaking French
  具法文說寫能力。

✦ German：fluent（reading, writing, speaking）
　德文：流利（讀、寫、説）

✦ English Word-processing：50wpm
　英文文字處理：每分鐘50字。

✦ Personal Computer：Experienced in JEC PC 9800
　個人電腦：熟悉 JEC PC 9800 電腦。

✦ Computer Language：BASIC, COBOL, FORTRAN
　電腦語言：BASIC, COBOL, FORTRAN.

✦ Have working knowledge of all common office machines
　Office skills include：typing 60 wpm, shorthand 90 wpm.
　對一般辦公室機器具備應用的知識
　辦公室技能包括：打字每分鐘60字、速記每分鐘90字。

著作・專利權（*Publications / Patents*）

　　如果曾經寫過和想應徵的工作有關的書或論文，將是履歷表中一個有利的參考事項，記得要列出書名或文章的名稱，刊載在何處，以及它的日期。

1　"Operating your office," published by China Post, March 4, 2008.
　辦公室管理，2008年3月4日發表於中國郵報。

2　"Macroeconomics for the 21st Century," a 500-page book, published in 2008 by Everyday Publishing Company, Taipei.
　二十一世紀總體經濟學，500頁，台北每日出版公司2008年印行。

　　和業務有關係的專利權，也是履歷表上很重要的一項，務必書寫清楚。

References 保證人

　　要不要寫上保證人，可以視情況而定。如果有一位有力的保證人，為了吸引雇主的注意，可以寫下來，否則，可以等雇主要求時再寫。以下都是可作為保證人的人選：

　　大學教授（學問及性格方面）

　　公司的上司（業務及個性方面）

　　其他的公司同仁（個性方面）

自己的親朋好友，通常不會對應徵者有不好的評語，所以不適合作為保證人。請別人作為你的保證人時，一定要**事先通知**他，讓他了解，並把履歷表的副本寄給他作參考。

　　可以像下面這樣，把保證人寫在最後面。

REFERENCES

Prof. Nan-Po Liu	Mr. Kuan-Ling Chao
Faculty of Commerce	Manager, Export Department
Taiwan University	Shonan Electric Co.
Taipei	Taipei
2304118	7082311

保　證　人

台灣大學	湘南電子公司（台北市）
商學院	出口部經理
劉南博教授	趙冠凌先生
2304118	7082311

　　如果同樣的履歷表要寄給多位雇主，就不要寫保證人，只要註明如下：

* References will be supplied upon request.
　　若需要保證人，將會提出。

　　有時我們考慮到下列狀況時，也會不寫保證人：

(1) 擔任保證人時，彼此一定要有某種程度的交談後，有了瞭解，才會答應。

(2) 擔任保證人，常會有雇主和他們聯絡，會造成人家不便。

(3) **有保證人並不見得有利**，也許雇主和保證人一談，反而失去了面談的機會，應該避免這種風險。

(4) 在履歷表有限的空間裏，應該寫上更重要的項目。

第三篇

英文履歷表的寫作技巧

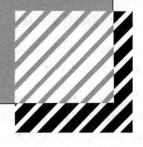

How to Write a Successful Resume

1.第一印象──格式

　　英文履歷表有各種形式，並不固定，完全是自由使用，但是以強調重點的差異，最主要有下列三種：

(1) 以**學歷**為主的履歷表（ *Basic resume* ）

　　適用於剛剛畢業或經歷較少的人，時間上是由最近往回寫。

(2) 以**經歷**為主的履歷表（ *Chronological resume* ）

　　把和應徵工作有關的經歷和業績，按順序書寫的形式。適合經歷多的人，但也要摘要說明自己的經歷，應徵高級職務時，可派上用場。

(3) 另一個也以經歷為主的履歷表，但和時間沒有關係（ *Functional resume* ）。它把一些特定的**職務集中**在一起，合併各種經驗，找出共通性；對一些需要特別技術的工作，強調出專門性；如果曾在一流的公司服務過，按公司不同寫出，也很有效果。

＊　　　　　＊　　　　　＊

　　依強調重點的不同，履歷表內項目也略有差異。在 Basic resume 中，包括下列項目，但仍可稍加變動：

① Name, address （ with postal number ）, telephone number.

　　姓名，住址（附郵遞區號），電話號碼。

② Personal Data — age, birthdate, birthplace, marital status, children, health, date of availability, etc.

　　個人資料──年齡，出生日期，出生地，婚姻狀況，兒女情形，健康狀態，可上班日期等等。

③ Objective / Job Objective / Career Objective
希望職務

④ Qualifications　資格

⑤ Education (honors, awards, etc.)
學歷 (榮譽 , 獎學金等等)

⑥ Extracurricular Activities 課外活動

⑦ Work Experience / Employment 經歷

⑧ Summer Jobs / Part-time Jobs 工讀

⑨ Language Proficiency 語文能力

⑩ Technical Qualifications 資格檢定考試

⑪ Special Skills 特殊才能

⑫ Hobbies / Interests 興趣

　　已踏入社會 , 有工作經驗的人 , 通常可以採用 Chronological resume , 讓雇主迅速地判斷你的能力及性向。它大致包括以下項目 :

① Name, address, telephone number
姓名、住址、電話號碼

② Objective / Job Objective 希望的職務

③ Qualifications 資格

④ Work Experience 經歷
包括 :

☆ 目前所服務工作或剛離職的公司要寫在最前面 , 並列出
　　‧公司的概況
　　‧所負責的工作
　　‧業績 (包括每種業務)

☆ 再寫出在目前所待的公司之前的公司 , 也要列出

- 公司的概況
- 所負責的工作
- 業績（包括各種業務）

這一部份也是按順序回寫到第一個服務的公司，如果是和希望應徵的職務沒有關係的經歷，或是很久以前的經歷，只要簡略說明即可。

⑤ Education 學歷

⑥ Extracurricular activities 課外活動

⑦ Technical Qulifications 資格檢定考試

⑧ Professional Memberships 專業技術的會員

⑨ Hobbies / Interests 興趣

Functional resume 強調某些特定工作的能力及適應程度，是以工作經驗為主。但這種形式的履歷表從企劃、管理、銷售等角度來加以整理，和某些公司的關連比較小，所以如果曾在一流的公司服務過，就要把公司名稱寫得醒目些。以下是可供參考的例子：

≪工作經驗≫

Functional Summary of Work Experience:

Corporate Planning:

Responsible for planning reorganization of corporate operation of Textile Division. Streamlined and vitalized global operation of the division.

General Management:

Responsible for operation of Textile 2nd Dep't.

Increased profit by 20% in 2004.

International Marketing:

Responsible for overseas sales of Textile 2nd Dep't.

Increased sales to North America by 20% in 2003.

工作經驗的職務概述：

組織計畫：

　負責紡織部門組織經營的重組計畫。部門全體經營的效率化
　及生動化。

總管理：

　負責經營紡織第二部門。2004年增加20％的利益。

國際市場：

　負責紡織第二部門的海外銷售。2003年對北美銷售增加
　20％。

──≪工作經驗≫──

Work Covered:

　Curriculum administration. Selected and developed
　teaching materials. Designed a teaching schedule for
　children, which was employed in the language insti-
　tute worked for, 2008.

工作涵蓋：

　課程管理。選擇及發展教材。爲兒童設計一份教學進度表，
　爲所工作的語言機構採用，2008年。

 # 寫英文履歷表的準備工作

　在準備動手寫英文履歷表時，可以遵循下列步驟：

- ✤ 蒐集原始資料：幫助自己決定履歷表的焦點，和處理及書寫的方法。
- ✤ 整理資料。
- ✤ 選出關係密切的資料。
- ✤ 用適當的語句把資料表現在履歷表上，也就是簡單、明瞭。
- ✤ 選擇履歷表的格式。

✠ 考慮履歷表的大小。

✠ 開始著手進行。

 # 英文履歷表的打字

　　履歷表一定要讓人覺得容易閱讀，因此履歷表的體裁及打字的好壞，對雇主對你的第一印象有很大的影響。下面是幾個要點：

✠ 用 A4 的白紙。

✠ 如果沒有指定用手寫，則使用電腦打字。儘量使用品質良好的印表機，而且墨色要均勻。

✠ 必須有效利用左右上下及行間空白的地方，左右至少各留兩公分，上下至少各留二點五公分，而且每個項目都要空行。

✠ 如果整齊且易於閱讀的話，也可以用影印的；凸版印刷同樣也有很好的效果。

✠ 絕對避免任何的錯誤。

✠ 強調構成要素，可以使用**大寫字體**，或者**底下畫線**的方式。

✠ 每一段要儘量**簡短**，段落之間空一至二行。給予適當距離的兩頁履歷表，比一頁但卻密密麻麻的履歷表容易閱讀。如果是兩頁的話，在每一頁最上方的位置，要寫上姓名及頁碼。

 # 參考格式

　　以下有六式履歷表格式可供參考。前四式是平常的版面，後面二式屬於個人的自由創作，現在也愈來愈多人使用。若雇主要求，也可貼上照片。

(一)

(二)

(三)

(四)

(五)

RESUME	
NAME * Marie Lee	BIRTHDATE * April 28, 1984

HEALTH*Excellent	SEX*Female	Marital Status*Single

ADDRESS * 326 Chung Hua Road, Taipei 10513
　　　　　　7049233

DATE	EDUCATION
September 2005-Present	Taiwan University, Department of Management Major:　Accounting Others: Business Administration, Data 　　　　　Processing Financial Management
September 2002-2005	Tainan Girls' High School, Tainan Member of Computer Science Club

CERTIFICATES	* Abucus Calculation 2nd class, 2004 * National Ordinary Examination, 2005

EXPERIENCE	* Salesgirl at Happy Record Shop, 　summer, 2006 * Salesgirl at Daily Fast Food Shop, 　summer, 2005 * Clerk (cash register) at Liberty 　Department Store, part-time, 2004

HOBBIES	* Computer games * Wordprocessing * Taking pictures of wild flowers

(六)

RESUME		
NAME * Mary Lin	AGE * 23	SINGLE
ADDRESS * 488 Chung Hsiao West Road, Taipei		
TEL * 8513341	Birthday * December 7, 1985	

EDUCATION	September 2004-Present	* Chenchi University Faculty of Management Accounting Major Courses taken: Accounting Bookkeeping, Management, Computer Programming
	September 2001-2004	* Taipei Girls' High School, Taipei

LICENCE	Abacus Caculation 2nd class, 2004 Driver's license, 2005
PART-TIME JOB	Salesgirl at a bakery shop, two days a week, 2006 Waitress at a restaurant, one day a week, 2005 Cashier at a convenience store, one day a week, 2004
HOBBIES	Reading novels Listening to modern music---rock and pops Sports---volleyball, tennis, and swimming

How to Write A Successful Resume

2.常用的資格及職務說法

● 求才廣告上常見的資格限制

☺ A cheerful character with strong secretarial and managerial and people skills is essential.

☺ 須個性開朗，祕書及管理能力強,具人際關係技巧。

☺ A desirable candidate should be eager to learn and have no allergy to computers.

☺ 應試者須熱心學習且能接觸電腦。

☺ A good understanding and working knowledge of computers is essential.

☺ 須具電腦理解及應用的知識。

☺ A person with ability plus flexibility should apply.

☺ 需要有能力及適應力強的人。

☺ A stable personality and high sense of responsibility are desirable.

☺ 須個性穩定、具高度責任感。

☺ An excellent understanding of English would be mandatory.

☺ 須具極好英文理解能力。

＊＊ mandatory〔ˈmændə͵tɔrɪ〕 *adj.* 命令的；強迫性的

୧ Ability to communicate in English desirable.

୧ 須英文溝通能力強。

୧ Above-average English / Japanese communications, organizational ability.

୧ 一般水準以上的英 / 日語溝通及組織能力。

୧ Absolutely must have a technical degree and extensive experience in computers.

୧ 須具備專門技術學位及豐富的電腦經驗。

---

୧ Accountants experienced in Western-style cost and management accounting plus all-round English and computer skills.

୧ 會計員，對西式成本及管理會計有經驗，並備精湛的英語能力及電腦技能。

୧ Accurate typing / English speaking ability required.

୧ 須打字正確 / 英語說講能力。

---

୧ Active sales staff who can be available for business trips abroad.

୧ 積極的銷售人員，能夠到國外出差者。

୧ Age under 25 preferable but not absolute condition.

୧ 二十五歲以下者尤佳，但並非必然條件。

୧ Ambitious attitude essential.

୧ 須具有野心。

** cost accounting 成本會計

ଓ Applicant must show initiative and work under pressure of deadlines.

ଓ 應徵者須積極進取並能在期限的壓力下工作。

ଓ Bank experience welcome.

ଓ 歡迎有銀行實務經驗的人。

ଓ Basic English and interpersonal skills essential.

ଓ 須備基本的英語能力及人際關係技巧。

ଓ Bilingual, typing 60 wpm, shorthand 90 wpm, dictaphone essential.

ଓ 須會兩種語言、打字每分鐘六十個字、速記每分鐘九十個字,並熟悉錄音抄寫。

ଓ Bright, aggressive applicants.

ଓ 須聰明、積極的應徵者。

ଓ Candidate must be bilingual, reliable, outgoing and tough-minded.

ଓ 應試者須會兩種語言、負責可靠、善交際且講求實際。

ଓ Candidate should have ability to transcribe dication.

ଓ 應試者須能譯寫聽寫內容。

ଓ Candidates should be willing to assume responsibilities.

ଓ 應試者須願意擔當責任。

ଓ Candidates who have a general knowledge of economics and a self motivated personality will be most suitable.

ଓ 具有一般的經濟學知識及個性主動的應試者最佳。

** biligual〔baɪˈlɪŋgwəl〕*adj.* 能說兩種語言的
dictaphone〔ˈdɪktəˌfon〕*n.* 錄音機;口授留聲機
transcribe〔trænˈskraɪb〕*v.* 用另一種文字或符號寫出

ප Cheerful person, conversant with all secretarial skills including typing, operating wordprocessor.

ප 個性開朗、精通各種祕書技能，包括打字及文字處理操作。

ප Efficient secretary with initiative aged between 28－33 required.

ප 徵有能力的祕書，須積極進取，年齡28－33歲。

ප Energetic, fashion minded person required.

ප 須積極、思想新潮者。

ප Enthusiasm, organized work-habits more important than experience.

ප 有熱誠，井然有序的工作習慣，經驗不拘。

ප Engineering degree desirable but not mandatory if good technical related experience.

ප 須具工程學位，如有相關的工業技術經驗亦可。

ප English wordprocessor capability preferable.

ප 有英語文字處理能力者優先。

ප Excellent secretarial skills and ability to deal with clients considered important.

ප 必須具備極佳的祕書技能及與客戶往來之能力。

ප Experience shipping-loading duties highly welcome.

ප 非常歡迎有船貨職務經驗的人。

** conversant〔ˈkɑnvɚsṇt, kənˈvɚsṇt〕*adj.* 精通的
　　client〔ˈklaɪənt〕*n.*（律師或專門職業的）委託人；（商店的）顧客

⊳ Experience in typing, telex, computer/wordprocessor and good command of English essential.

⊳ 須具有打字、商務電報、電腦／文字處理經驗並精通英文。

⊳ Experience in handling practical business details of fixed assests is a must.

⊳ 須有處理固定資產實務細節之經驗。

⊳ Experience working in multinational environment helpful.

⊳ 有在多國環境下工作的經驗者尤佳。

⊳ Extensive experience in administrative accounting a must.

⊳ 須具管理會計方面的廣泛經驗。

⊳ Familiarity with or interest in international trade issues a major plus.

⊳ 必須熟悉或對國際貿易問題有興趣者更佳。

⊳ Flexible, aggressive and attentive person is wanted.

⊳ 須適應力強、積極認真者。

⊳ Fluency in spoken English is a major requirement.

⊳ 主要條件為英語說講流利。

⊳ Fluency in oral and written English, experience of senior clerical job in computer related department essential.

⊳ 須英語說寫流利，在電腦相關部門擔任高級書記的工作經驗。

** assests〔ˋæsɛts〕*n.* 財產；資產　multinational〔͵mʌltɪˋnæʃən!〕*adj.* 多國的
clerical〔ˋklɛrɪk!〕*adj.* 辦事員的；書記的

ཚ Good command of English, typing（minimum 60 wpm）and telex required, also preferably wordprocessing.

ཚ 須熟諳英語，打字（每分鐘最少60個字），及商務電報，懂文字處理者尤佳。

ཚ Good command of English with ability to understand handwritten English required.

ཚ 須熟諳英語能看懂手寫英語。

ཚ Good command of English both verbal and written, over 3 years experience in any international business.

ཚ 英文說寫能力強，有三年以上任何國際貿易經驗。

ཚ Good English, accurate typing skills, correspondence, and over 3 years experience in any well-organized company.

ཚ 英文佳、打字正確、信函處理，並在組織健全的公司工作經驗達三年以上。

ཚ Good English and calculation skills are necessary.

ཚ 須英語及計算能力佳。

ཚ Good personality with excellent typing ability desired.

ཚ 須個性良好、具一流的打字能力。

ཚ Good phone manners required.

ཚ 須有良好的電話禮貌。

ཚ Good typing, telex, filing, and general secretarial skills needed.

ཚ 須熟打字、商務電報、檔案處理及一般祕書技巧。

ප Highly energetic, mature, bal-
anced, competitive team
members.

ප 相當積極、成熟、有條不
紊、不怕競爭的組員。

ප Highly-motivated and reliable
person with excellent health
and pleasant personality.

ප 企圖心強又可靠者，並且
非常健康、個性開朗。

ප IC/Systems design experience
background recommended.

ප 具 I C／系統設計經驗尤
佳。

ප Interpersonal skills required.

ප 須備人際關係技巧。

ප Knowledge of microcomputer
and software programming
would be advantageous.

ප 具微電腦及軟體程式方面
知識者尤佳。

ප Knowledge of U.S. specifications and standards a plus.

ප 具美國規格標準方面知識
者尤佳。

ප Market oriented staffer with
knowledge of shipping docu-
mentation and some technical
background.

ප 市場銷售方面職員，具備
裝船文件知識以及一些專
業經歷。

ප Must have experience in international sales and ability to
produce results.

ප 須具國際銷售經驗及創造
業績之能力。

＊＊ specifications〔͵spɛsəfə'keʃən〕 *n.* 規格

ಆ Marketing experience helpful
but not essential.

ಆ 具市場經驗尤佳,無亦可。

ಆ Must be able to handle all
international communications
in English.

ಆ 必須能用英文處理所有的
國際書信、電訊。

ಆ Must be sharp, possess com-
municative skills, and a fast
learner.

ಆ 須敏銳、有溝通技巧、學
習能力強。

ಆ Only person willing to progress
should apply.

ಆ 須有進步意願者。

ಆ Organized hardworker with
background in marketing.

ಆ 有條不紊的勤奮工作者,
具市場經驗。

ಆ Pleasant telephone manner and
excellent English comprehension
required.

ಆ 須具合宜的電話禮貌、極
好的英文理解能力。

ಆ Pleasantly aggressive, bilingual
with Marketing/Sales/Organi-
zational awareness.

ಆ 開朗積極、會兩種語言、
有市場／銷售／組織意識。

ಆ Positive/active mind essential.

ಆ 須有積極／靈活的頭腦。

ಆ Practical English language
proficiency and accurate typing
skills.

ಆ 精通實用英語、打字正確。

ひ Preference given to person experienced in shipping.

ひ 有船運經驗者優先。

ひ Previous bank experience would be an advantage.

ひ 先前有銀行實務經驗者優先。

ひ Previous experience in a foreign capital company an asset.

ひ 具外資公司經驗者尤佳。

ひ Proven skills in typing, transcription, and wordprocessor / computer, telephone operation, administrative and secretarial duties.

ひ 在打字、謄寫、文字處理／電腦、電話操作、行政及祕書職務的技能方面有經驗。

ひ Someone willing to learn and progress.

ひ 肯學習且向上進取者。

ひ Should have good command of English and reasonable typing skill.

ひ 須熟諳英文、具一般打字技巧。

ひ Secretary with good English knowledge and accounting experience.

ひ 徵祕書，英文佳、具會計經驗。

ひ Some familiarity with personal computers required.

ひ 須略為熟悉個人電腦。

ひ Some typing ability preferable.

ひ 略具打字能力者優先。

❸ Some secretarial experience and a cooperative personality are musts.

❸ 須略具祕書經驗、個性合作。

❸ Self-starter, familiarity with database. Willing to work in bilingual situation with latest OA equipment.

❸ 自動自發、熟資料管理。願在具最新ＯＡ系統的雙語言環境工作者。

---

❸ The candidate should be a bright, highly motivated, well organized individual.

❸ 應試者必須是個反應快，企圖心強、組織能力良好的人。

❸ The main qualities required are preparedness to work hard, ability to learn, ambition and good health.

❸ 主要必備特質是要能預備工作勤奮、有學習能力、有野心及健康良好。

❸ Translation, word processor, filing skills necessary.

❸ 須翻譯、文字處理及檔案處理技巧。

---

❸ Working command of spoken & written English.

❸ 應用英文說寫能力。

❸ Working experience and fluency in English desirable.

❸ 須工作經驗及英文流利。

❸ Young, bright, energetic, bilingual with good people-skills, career-ambition.

❸ 年輕、聰明、有活力，會兩種語，具良好人際關係技巧及事業野心。

♤ 求才廣告上常見的職務

Account Executive	（廣告或服務業的）業務經理
Accountant〔ə'kaʊntənt〕	會計員
Accounting Assistant	會計助理
Accounting Clerk	記帳員
Accounting Manager	會計部經理
Accounting Secretary	會計書記
Accounting Staff	會計人員

♧   ♧   ♧

Accounting Supervisor	會計主管
Administration Manager	行政經理
Administration Staff	行政人員
Administrative Assistant	行政助理
Administrative Clerk	行政辦事員
Administrative Coordinator	行政協調人員
Administrative Staff	行政人員

♧   ♧   ♧

Administrator〔əd'mɪnə,stretɚ〕	管理者；行政官
Advertising Staff	廣告工作人員
Airlines Sales Representative	航空公司機票定位人員
Airlines Staff	航空公司職員
Analyst〔'ænḷɪst〕	分析者；分析家
Application Engineer	應用工程師
Architect〔'ɑrkə,tɛkt〕	建築師

Bond Analyst ──────── 證券分析人

Bond Dealer ──────── 證券交易人

Bond Trader ──────── 證券交易人

Bookkeeper 〔'bʊk͵kipɚ〕──── 簿記員

Business Controller ──────── 業務主任

Business Manager ──────── 業務經理

Buyer 〔'baɪɚ〕──────（大百貨公司或其他機構之）專管採買之人

♤　　　　　♤　　．　　♤

Cardmember Service Rep. ──────── 卡片會員服務代表

Certified Public Account ──────── 檢定合格會計師

Chemist 〔'kɛmɪst〕──────── 藥劑師；藥商

Chief Accountant ──────── 會計主任

Civil Engineer ──────── 土木工程師

Clerk 〔klɝk〕──────── 文書；辦事員

Clerk / Receptionist ──────── 店員／招待員

Clerk Typist ──────── 文書打字

Clerk Typist & Secretary ──────── 文書打字兼祕書

♤　　　　　♤　　　　　♤

Comptroller 〔kən'trolɚ〕──────── 主計，會計主任

Computer Data Input Operator ──────── 電腦程式輸入員

Computer Engineer ──────── 電腦工程師

Computer Processing Operator ──────── 電腦處理操作員

Computer System Manager ──────── 電腦系統經理

Computer Training Staff ──────── 電腦訓練人員

Computer Translator ──────── 電腦翻譯員

Controller 〔kən'trolɚ〕──────── 主計員；（大機關裏的）組、處主任

Coordinator〔koˈɔrdəˌnetɚ〕————— 協調人
Coordinator / Researcher ————— 協調人 / 研究員
Copy Editor ————————— 編輯；改寫者
Copy Reader ————————— 校訂人；原稿之訂正與編輯者
Copywriter〔ˈkɑpɪˌraɪtɚ〕——— 廣告文字撰稿人
Counselor〔ˈkaʊnslɚ〕————— 法律顧問；律師

♤　　　　　　♤　　　　　　♤

Counselor / Coordinator ————— 顧問 / 協調者
Credit Analyst ————————— 信譽調查員
Data Processing Clerk ————— 資料處理人員
Dealer〔ˈdilɚ〕——————— 商人；交易人
Distribution Coordinator———— 產銷協調者
EDP Auditor ————————— 電子資料處理稽核員
EDP Manager ————————— 電子資料處理經理
Economic Research Assistant ——— 經濟研究助理
Editor〔ˈɛdɪtɚ〕——————— 編輯；主筆

♤　　　　　　♤　　　　　　♤

Editor / Coordinator ————— 編輯 / 協調者
Editorial Assistant ————— 助理編輯
Electrical Engineer ————— 電機工程師
Electronics Staff ————— 電子人員
Engineer〔ˌɛndʒəˈnɪr〕——— 機械師；技師；工程師
Engineering Technician ——— 工程技師
English Instructor ————— 英語教師
Export Clerk ————————— 出口人員
Export Sales Manager ———— 外銷部經理

Export Sales Staff ——————————— 外銷部職員
Export Secretary ——————————— 外銷部祕書
Executive Interpreter ——————————— 執行翻譯
Executive Secretary ——————————— 執行祕書
Finance Executive ——————————— 財政計劃釐定人
Financial Controller ——————————— 財務主任
Financial Reporter ——————————— 財務報告人
FX (Foreign Exchange) Clerk ——————————— 外滙職員
FX Settlement Clerk ——————————— 外滙清算人員

♤　　　　　♤　　　　　♤

Free-lance Translator ——————————— 自由翻譯者
Free-lance Writer ——————————— 自由作家
Fund Manager ——————————— 財務經理
General Administration ——————————— 總行政
General Auditor ——————————— 審計長
General Manager ——————————— 總經理
Ground Hostess ——————————— 女地勤人員
Hardware Engineer ——————————— 硬體工程師

♤　　　　　♤　　　　　♤

Import Coordinator ——————————— 進口協調人
Import Liaison Staff ——————————— 進口聯絡員
Insurance Actuary ——————————— 保險公司的核計員；理賠員
Internal Auditor ——————————— 國內查帳員
International Grain Trader ——————————— 國際穀物貿易商
International Marketing ——————————— 國際市場交易
International Sales Staff ——————————— 國際行銷人員

Interior Staff	內政人員
Interpreter 〔ɪn'tɝprɪtɚ〕	口譯員
Junior Secretary	中級祕書
Law Office Secretary	法務祕書
Librarian 〔laɪ'brɛrɪən〕	圖書館員
Line Supervisor	生產線上管理者
Maintenance Engineer	維護工程師
Management Consultant	管理顧問

♠ ♠ ♠

Management Coordinator	管理協調者
Manager 〔'mænɪdʒɚ〕	經理
Manufacturing Engineer	製造工程師
Manufacturing Worker	生產員工
Market Analyst	市場分析家
Market Development Manager	市場開發經理
Marketing Manager	市場銷售經理
Marketing Staff	市場銷售人員

♠ ♠ ♠

Market Oriented Staffer	市場銷售人員
Marketing Assistant	銷售助理
Marketing Executive	行銷主管
Marketing Officer	銷售人員
Marketing Personnel	銷售人員
Marketing Representative	銷售代表
Marketing Research Manager	市場研究經理
Mechanical Engineer	機械工程師

Money Market Dealer ——————— 金融業者
Music Teacher ————————— 音樂老師
Office Accountant ——————— 會　計
Office Assistant / Manager ——— 助理／經理
Office Clerk ————————— 職員；辦事員
Office Staff ————————— 職　員
Office Worker ————————— 職　員

♤　　　　　♤　　　　　♤

Operational Manager ————— 管理經理
Operations Clerk ——————— 操作員
Package Designer ——————— 包裝設計人
Passenger Reservation Staff ——— 負責預定乘客票位的職員
Personnel Clerk ——————— 人事部職員
Personnel Staff ——————— 人事部職員
Pharmacist〔'farməsɪst〕——— 藥劑師
Placement Coordinator ———— 配置協調人
Planner〔'plænɚ〕————— 設計者；策畫人
Plant Manager ——————— 廠　長

♤　　　　　♤　　　　　♤

Private Secretary ——————— 私人祕書
Product Manager ——————— 生產部經理
Production Control Specialist ——— 生產管制專家
Production Engineer ————— 生產技師
Professional Staff ————— 專業人員
Programmer〔'progræmɚ〕———— 電腦程式設計人
Project Staff ————————— 策畫人員

Promotional Manager ———————— 推廣部經理
Proofreader〔ˈprufˌridɚ〕———————— 校對員
Purchasing Agent ———————— 購買經紀人（進貨員）
Real Estate Staff ———————— 不動產人員
Receptionist〔rɪˈsɛpʃənɪst〕———————— 招待員
Receptionist － Clerk ———————— 招待員－店員
Receptionist － Telephonist ———————— 招待員－接線生
Receptionist － Typist ———————— 招待員－打字員

♤　　　　　♤　　　　　♤

Recruitment Coordinator ———————— 招募協調人
Regional Manager ———————— 區域經理
Remittance Clerk ———————— 滙款職員
Representative〔ˌrɛprɪˈzɛntətɪv〕———————— 代　表
Reporter〔rɪˈpɔrtɚ〕———————— 記者；通訊員
R & D Engineer ———————— 研究開發技師

♤　　　　　♤　　　　　♤

Research Assistant ———————— 研究助理
Research Trainee ———————— 研究見習生
Researcher〔rɪˈsɝtʃɚ〕———————— 研究人員
Restaurant Manager ———————— 餐廳經理
Rewrite Person ———————— 做報紙改寫工作的編輯或記者
Sales Administation Clerk ———————— 銷售行政人員
Sales and Planning Staff ———————— 銷售計畫員
Sales Assistant ———————— 銷售助理
Sales Clerk ———————— 店員；售貨員
Sales Coordinator ———————— 銷售協調者

Sales Engineer ─────────── 銷售技師

Sales Executive ─────────── 行銷主管

Sales Liaison Staffer ─────── 銷售連絡人

Sales Manager ─────────── 銷售部經理

Salesperson〔'selzpɝsn̩〕───── 銷售員；店員

Sales Promotion Manager ───── 銷售推廣部經理

♠ ♠ ♠

Sales Representative ─────── 銷售代表

Sales Superviser ────────── 銷售管理者

School Registrar ────────── 學校註冊主任

Secretarial Assistant ─────── 祕書助理

Secretarial Clerk ──────── 祕 書

Secretary〔'sɛkrə,tɛrɪ〕────── 祕 書

Secretary / Office Clerk ───── 祕書／辦事員

Secretary / Receptionist ───── 祕書／招待員

Securities Custody Clerk ───── 保安人員

♠ ♠ ♠

Security Officer ────────── 安全人員

Senior Accountant ──────── 高級會計員

Senior Consultant ──────── 高級顧問

Senior Secretary ────────── 高級祕書

Service Manager ────────── 服務部經理

Settlement Clerk ────────── 清算人員

Shipping Clerk ──────────── 負責貨務打包及裝運之人

Shop Coordinator ────────── 商店經理

Simultaneous Interpreter ───── 同步翻譯員

Software Engineer ——————————— 軟體工程師

Staff Assistant ——————————— 助　理

Staff Engineer ——————————— 工　程　師

Supervisor〔ˌsjupə'vaɪzə〕——————— 監督者；管理人

Systems Adviser ——————————— 系統顧問

Systems Engineer ——————————— 系統工程師

Systems Operator ——————————— 系統操作員

Technical Editor ——————————— 具技術知識的編輯

♤　　　　　　　♤　　　　　　　♤

Technical Liaison ——————————— 技術連絡

Technical Liaison Manager ——————— 技術連絡經理

Technical Management ——————————— 技術管理

Technical Translator ——————————— 具技術知識的翻譯

Telecommunication Executive ————— 電訊員；電信員

Telex Operator ——————————— 打字電報操縱員

Telex / Postal Clerk ——————————— 打字電報 / 郵政人員

Trade Finance Executive ————————— 進出口財務主管

♤　　　　　　　♤　　　　　　　♤

Trainee Managers ——————————— 管理受訓人員的經理

Translation Checker ——————————— 翻譯核對員

Translator〔træns'letə〕——————— 翻　譯　員

Trust Banking Executive ——————— 銀行高級職員

Typing / Shipping Clerk ——————————— 打字 / 送貨員

Typist〔'taɪpɪst〕——————————— 打　字　員

Wordprocessor Operator ——————————— 文字處理操作員

How to Write a Successful Resume

3. 遣詞用字的技巧

㈠ 使用主動積極的語彙

寫英文履歷表時，使用以下語彙，可以達到更好的效果。

- □ **accelerated** 〔 æk'sɛlə,retɪd 〕 *adj.* 加速的；速成的
- □ **accomplished** 〔 ə'kɑmplɪʃt 〕 *adj.* 完善的；熟練的
- □ **achieved** 〔 ə'tʃivd 〕 *adj.* 完成的；達成的
- □ **adapted** 〔 ə'dæptɪd 〕 *adj.* 適應的
- □ **administered** 〔 əd'mɪnəstəd 〕 *adj.* 管理的；執行的
- □ **analyzed** 〔 'ænḷ,aɪzd 〕 *adj.* 分析的
- □ **approved** 〔 ə'pruvd 〕 *adj.* 核准的；證明過的
- □ **arranged** 〔 ə'rendʒd 〕 *adj.* 排列好的
- □ **assisted** 〔 ə'sɪstɪd 〕 *adj.* 輔助的

※※ ————————————————

- □ **clarified** 〔 'klærə,faɪd 〕 *adj.* 明確的；澄清的
- □ **completed** 〔 kəm'plitɪd 〕 *adj.* 完成的；完整的
- □ **conceived** 〔 kən'sivd 〕 *adj.* 構思的；表達的
- □ **conducted** 〔 kən'dʌktɪd 〕 *adj.* 經營的；領導的
- □ **correlated** 〔 'kɔrə,letɪd 〕 *adj.* 相關連的
- □ **created** 〔 krɪ'etɪd 〕 *adj.* 創造的
- □ **delegated** 〔 'dɛlə,getɪd 〕 *adj.* 委託的；授權的
- □ **demonstrated** 〔 'dɛmən,stretɪd 〕 *adj.* 示範的；證實的
- □ **designed** 〔 dɪ'zaɪnd 〕 *adj.* 計畫的；原意的

□ **developed** 〔 dɪ'vɛləpt 〕 *adj.* 發展的；已開發的

□ **devised** 〔 dɪ'vaɪzd 〕 *adj.* 設計出的；發明的

□ **directed** 〔 də'rɛktɪd 〕 *adj.* 經管理的；受督導的

□ **doubled** 〔 'dʌbḷd 〕 *adj.* 加倍的；雙重的

□ **earned** 〔 ɝnd 〕 *adj.* 獲得的；賺取的

□ **effected** 〔 ə'fɛktɪd 〕 *adj.* 實現的

□ **eliminated** 〔 ɪ'lɪmə,netɪd 〕 *adj.* 剔除的；削減的

□ **enlarged** 〔 ɪn'lɑrdʒd 〕 *adj.* 擴充的；增大的

※※ ─────────────────────

□ **established** 〔 ə'stæblɪʃt 〕 *adj.* 已設立的；確立的

□ **evaluated** 〔 ɪ'væljʊ,etɪd 〕 *adj.* 評估的

□ **executed** 〔 'ɛksɪ,kjutɪd 〕 *adj.* 執行的；實施的

□ **expanded** 〔 ɪk'spændɪd 〕 *adj.* 擴展的；膨脹的

□ **expedited** 〔 'ɛkspɪ,daɪtɪd 〕 *adj.* 加速的

□ **formed** 〔 fɔrmd 〕 *adj.* 構成的；形成的

□ **founded** 〔 'faʊndɪd 〕 *adj.* 創設的；建立的

□ **generated** 〔 'dʒɛnə,retɪd 〕 *adj.* 造成的；生產的

□ **guided** 〔 'gaɪdɪd 〕 *adj.* 引領的；控制的

※※ ─────────────────────

□ **halved** 〔 hævd 〕 *adj.* 減半的

□ **headed** 〔 'hɛdɪd 〕 *adj.* 領導的

□ **implemented** 〔 'ɪmplə,mɛntɪd 〕 *adj.* 實施的；生效的

□ **improved** 〔 ɪm'pruvd 〕 *adj.* 改良的；改善的

□ **increased** 〔 ɪn'krist 〕 *adj.* 增加的；更多的

□ **influenced** 〔 'ɪnflʊənst 〕 *adj.* 受影響的；改變的

□ **initiated** 〔 ɪ'nɪʃɪ,etɪd 〕 *adj.* 創始的；發起的

□ **innovated** 〔 'ɪnə,vetɪd 〕 *adj.* 改革的；革新的

- **inspired** 〔 ɪn'spaɪrd 〕 *adj.* 受啓發的；受鼓舞的
- **installed** 〔 ɪn'stɔld 〕 *adj.* 安置的；裝設的
- **integrated** 〔 'ɪntə,gretɪd 〕 *adj.* 整體的；統合的
- **invented** 〔 ɪn'vɛntɪd 〕 *adj.* 發明的；創作的
- **justified** 〔 'dʒʌstə,faɪd 〕 *adj.* 經證明的；合法化的
- **launched** 〔 lɔntʃt 〕 *adj.* 開始的；著手的
- **led** 〔 lɛd 〕 *adj.* 被領導的；受控制的

✳✳ ─────────────────

- **managed** 〔 'mænɪdʒd 〕 *adj.* 受支配的；被管理的
- **maintained** 〔 men'tend 〕 *adj.* 堅持的；維護的
- **mastered** 〔 'mæstəd 〕 *adj.* 精通的；征服的
- **mediated** 〔 'midɪ,etɪd 〕 *adj.* 調停的；斡旋的
- **motivated** 〔 'motə,vetɪd 〕 *adj.* 激發的；誘導的
- **negotiated** 〔 nɪ'goʃɪ,etɪd 〕 *adj.* 交涉的；協議的
- **nominated** 〔 'nɑmə,netɪd 〕 *adj.* 被提名的；被任命的
- **operated** 〔 'ɑpə,retɪd 〕 *adj.* 操縱的；運轉的
- **ordered** 〔 'ɔrdəd 〕 *adj.* 下命令的；整頓的
- **originated** 〔 ə'rɪdʒə,netɪd 〕 *adj.* 創始的；發明的

✳✳ ─────────────────

- **organized** 〔 'ɔrgən,aɪzd 〕 *adj.* 有組織的
- **overcomed** 〔 ,ovə'kʌmd 〕 *adj.* 克服的；壓倒的
- **participated** 〔 pə'tɪsə,petɪd 〕 *adj.* 分享的；參與的
- **performed** 〔 pə'fɔrmd 〕 *adj.* 履行的；執行的
- **planned** 〔 plænd 〕 *adj.* 計畫的；預期的
- **prepared** 〔 prɪ'pɛrd 〕 *adj.* 預備的；準備的
- **presented** 〔 prɪ'zɛntɪd 〕 *adj.* 提出的；呈遞的
- **produced** 〔 prə'djust 〕 *adj.* 製造出的；生產的

- □ **promoted** 〔 prəˈmotɪd 〕 *adj.* 提倡的；促進的
- □ **proposed** 〔 prəˈpozd 〕 *adj.* 提議的；推薦的
- □ **provided** 〔 prəˈvaɪdɪd 〕 *adj.* 供應的；供給的
- □ **raised** 〔 rezd 〕 *adj.* 擢升的；提高的
- □ **recommended** 〔 ˌrɛkəˈmɛndɪd 〕 *adj.* 推薦的；介紹的
- □ **reconciled** 〔 ˈrɛkənˌsaɪld 〕 *adj.* 調停的；和解的
- □ **recorded** 〔 rɪˈkɔrdɪd 〕 *adj.* 記錄的；記載的
- □ **reduced** 〔 rɪˈdjust 〕 *adj.* 減縮的；減少的

※※ ─────────────────────

- □ **reinforced** 〔 ˌriɪnˈforst 〕 *adj.* 增強的；增援的
- □ **reorganized** 〔 riˈɔrgəˌnaɪzd 〕 *adj.* 改組的；改編的
- □ **reported** 〔 rɪˈportɪd 〕 *adj.* 報告的；報導的
- □ **researched** 〔 rɪˈsɝtʃt 〕 *adj.* 研究的；探索的
- □ **revised** 〔 rɪˈvaɪzd 〕 *adj.* 改正的；校訂的
- □ **reviewed** 〔 rɪˈvjud 〕 *adj.* 回顧的；檢討的
- □ **simplified** 〔 ˈsɪmpḷəˌfaɪd 〕 *adj.* 簡化的
- □ **solved** 〔 salvd 〕 *adj.* 解決的；解答的

※※ ─────────────────────

- □ **streamlined** 〔 ˈstrimˌlaɪnd 〕 *adj.* 改進的；有效率的
- □ **strengthened** 〔 ˈstrɛŋθənd 〕 *adj.* 強化的
- □ **succeeded** 〔 səkˈsidɪd 〕 *adj.* 成功的
- □ **supervised** 〔 ˌsupɚˈvaɪzd 〕 *adj.* 監督的；管理的
- □ **transformed** 〔 trænsˈformd 〕 *adj.* 變形的；改觀的
- □ **trained** 〔 trend 〕 *adj.* 受訓練的
- □ **unified** 〔 ˈjunəˌfaɪd 〕 *adj.* 統一的；合一的
- □ **verified** 〔 ˈvɛrəˌfaɪd 〕 *adj.* 經證實的；證明的

(二)表達出你所希望的職務

ප A position as data-processing manager that will enable me to use my knowledge of computer systems.

ප 資料處理經理的職務,能讓我運用電腦系統的知識。

ප A position in management training programs with the eventual goal of participating in the management phase of marketing.

ප 在管理訓練計畫方面的職務,最終目標在參與市場的管理層面。

ප A position which would utilize my educational background in marketing, with opportunities for advancement.

ප 能運用我在市場學方面的學歷,並有擢升的機會。

ප A position requiring analytical skills in the area of financial or investment field.

ප 在財務或投資領域,需運用分析技巧的職務。

ප A responsible administrative position that will provide challenge and freedom where I can use my initiative and creativity.

ප 負責行政的職位,提供挑戰和自由,使我能行使我的進取精神及創造能力。

** utilize〔'jutḷ‚aɪz〕v. 運用;使用
initiative〔ɪ'nɪʃɪ‚etɪv〕n. 進取精神

ↀ An entry-level position in sales.
Eventual goal : manager of
marketing department.

ↀ 在銷售方面的初級職位。
最終目標：市場部門的經
理。

ↀ An administrative secretarial
position where communication
skills and a pleasant attitude
toward people will be assets.

ↀ 行政祕書的職務，用得上
溝通技巧，及與人和善的
態度。

ↀ Acceptance in a management
training program.

ↀ 希望進入管理訓練計畫。

ↀ Administrative assistant to an
executive where shorthand and
typing skills, accuracy in handling details, and cheerful
personality will be assets.

ↀ 高級主管的行政助理：將
用上速記和打字技能，處
理細節精確，並且個性開
朗。

ↀ Entry-level position in an
accounting environment, which
ultimately leads to financial
management.

ↀ 會計部門的初級職位，最
後能夠管理財務。

ↀ Executive assistant position
utilizing interest, training and
experience in office administration.

ↀ 行政助理職務，運用辦公
室管理方面興趣、訓練及
經驗。

** asset〔ˈæset〕*n.* 有用的性質或技能

☺ Responsible entry-level position in computer programming.

☺ 負責電腦程式設計的初級職務。

☺ To begin as an accounting trainee and eventually become a manager.

☺ 從當會計見習生開始，最後成爲經理。

(三) 表達自己所具備的資格

☺ Ability to organize marketing campaigns and to supervise employees. Effective communication abilities.

☺ 能組織市場活動及督導員工。有效的溝通能力。

☺ Educational background in business administration with a major in secretarial science and two summers of fulltime work experience.

☺ 有企管的學歷，主修祕書學，兩個暑假的全職工作經驗。

☺ Five years of progressively more responsible experience in marketing, in addition to a bachelor's degree in management with major in marketing.

☺ 除了主修市場學的管理學學士學位，還有五年越來越負重責的市場貿易經驗。

☺ Six years of successful job experience ranging from sales responsibilities to management of marketing department.

☺ 六年的成功工作經驗，範圍則從銷售職責到市場部門的管理。

** trainee〔tre'ni〕*n.* 見習生

ප Special training in accounting at junior college and two years of practical experience in accounting environment.

ප 在二專受會計的特別訓練，而且在會計部門有兩年的實際經驗。

ප University education in management with an emphasis on accounting, involving the use of computers.

ප 在大學裏修管理學，以會計爲主，包含電腦的使用。

ප University major in marketing, two years of part-time sales experience, and proven ability to work with people.

ප 在大學主修市場學，兩年兼職的行銷經驗，而且有可以和人合作的表現。

ප University major in computer science, three years of part-time work in a computer software company.

ප 在大學主修電腦學，在電腦軟體公司兼差三年。

㈣ 說明自己的學歷

ප Academic preparation for general management：
　　Management：Principles of
　　　management, organization
　　　theory, behavioral science.
　　Accounting：Principles of
　　　accounting, cost analysis.

ප 大學時爲一般管理做的準備：
　管理學：管理學原理、組織理論、行爲科學。
　會計：會計原理、成本分析。

** academic〔͵ækə'dɛmɪk〕*adj.* 大學的；學術的

Communication : Business communication, personnel management, human relations.

Marketing : Marketing theory, sales management.

溝通：商務溝通、人事管理、人際關係。

市場學：市場學理論、行銷管理。

ඨ Among the pertinent courses I have taken are :

Operations research, data-processing, decision analysis, business statistics, multivariate analysis.

ඨ 在相關課程中我修過的有：操作研究、資料處理、決策分析、商用統計、變量分析。

ඨ Courses taken that would be useful for secretarial work :

Secretarial procedures, office administration, typing, business communication, data-processing, psychology.

ඨ 對祕書工作有用曾修過的課程：祕書程序、辦公室管理、打字、商務溝通、資料處理、心理學。

ඨ Intensive program covered all phases of secretarial work :

Basic secretarial theory, business correspondence, English typewriting, office management, data-processing.

ඨ 涵蓋各部分祕書工作的密集課程：祕書理論基礎、商務信函、英打、辦公室管理、資料處理。

ඨ Major courses contributing to management qualification :

Management, accounting, economics, marketing, sociology.

ඨ 對管理資格有幫助的主要課程：管理學、會計、經濟學、市場學、社會學。

** pertinent〔ˈpɝtn̩ənt〕*adj.* 和⋯有關的　contribute〔kənˈtrɪbjut〕*v.* 幫助；有助益

ᘓ Specialized courses pertaining
　to foreign trade：
　　Marketing principles, interna-
　　tional marketing, foreign trade
　　practice, foreign exchange,
　　business English.

ᘓ 和外貿相關的專門科目：
　市場學原理、國際市場、
　外貿實務、外滙滙兌、商
　用英文。

㈤ 工讀經驗的表達方法

ᘓ Earned 20 ％ of college expenses
　while working 25 hours weekly
　at accounting department of
　Far East Department Store.

ᘓ 在遠東百貨公司的會計部
　門工作時，每星期工作25
　小時，賺了大學費用的百
　分之二十。

ᘓ Full-time in summers, part-time
　during school.
　　Chia-Chia Restaurant. Started
　　as dish washer ; moved up to
　　assistant to Customer Service
　　Manager.

ᘓ 暑期全職，上課期間兼職。
　佳佳餐廳。從洗碗工當起，
　升到顧客服務經理的助理。

ᘓ Full-time summers and winters
　at 7-11 convenience store.
　　Responsibilities included
　　preparing data for inventory
　　control and making sales and
　　inventory reports. Earned 30%
　　of college expenses.

ᘓ 寒暑假在統一便利商店專
　任。
　職責包括準備存貨控制的
　資料，作銷售及存貨報告。
　賺了百分之三十的大學費
　用。

** *pertaining to* 和…有關　　inventory〔'ɪnvən,torɪ〕*n*. 存貨；清單

ප Practical summer business experience.
　Clerked at Royal clothing store in charge of sales, 2008.
　Employed at Huang family restaurant as waitress, 2006.

ප 實際的暑假職務經驗。
　2008 年，在皇家衣料店當店員，負責銷售。
　2006 年，在老黃餐館當女服務生。

㈥ 工作經歷

ප Administrative assistant to American executives.
　General secretarial activities, including planning conferences, doing research, assisting preparation of reports.

ප 美國高級主管的行政助理。一般祕書所做之事，包括安排會議、研究調查、協助準備報告。

ප Assistant to manager of accounting department of American-affiliated firm. Analyzed data into relevant financial statistics and produced monthly financial statements.

ප 美商公司會計部門經理的助理。分析與財務統計相關的資料，而且提出每月的財務報告。

ප Assistant to personnel manager. Responsible for hiring personnel and training employees. Wrote job description manual for all staff.

ප 人事經理的助理。負責招雇及訓練員工。為全體職員寫工作說明手冊。

** affiliate〔ə'fɪlɪˌet〕*v.* 密切關連
　statement〔'stetmənt〕*n.* 報告；說明

ଓ Computer programmer. Responsibilities include programming, checking validity of output and system malfunctions.

ଓ 電腦程式設計師。職責包括程式設計，檢查輸出系統的確實性及系統故障。

ଓ Manager of data-processing department. Selected data requirements, designed formats, and planned program specifications.

ଓ 資料處理部門的經理。選擇必要資料，設計表格形式，設計方案說明書。

ଓ Production manager : Initiated quality control resulting in a reduction in working hours by 15% while increasing productivity by 20%。

ଓ 生產部經理：着手品質管制，使得工作時數減少15%，生產力卻增加20%。

ଓ Reason for leaving : Professional and financial advancement offered by a promising organization.

ଓ 去職理由：提昇專業技術及財務情況，並由一家前途看好的機構所提供。

ଓ Sales manager. In addition to ordinary sales activities and management of department, responsible for recruiting and training of sales staff members.

ଓ 行銷部經理。除了一般銷售活動和部門管理之外，還負責吸收訓練銷售人員。

** malfunction〔mæl'fʌnkʃən〕*n.* 故障
specifications〔ˌspɛsəfə'keʃənz〕*n.* 規格；說明書
recruit〔rɪ'krut〕*v.* 吸收；招募

℘ Secretary to president of
American-affiliated firm.
Responsibilities：Receiving
visitors, scheduling meetings,
taking and typing dictation,
writing routine letters and
reports.

℘ 美商公司董事長祕書。
職責：接見訪客，安排會
議、筆錄並打字、
寫例行的信件及報
告。

℘ Secretary to manager of general
affairs at a foreign firm.
Responsibilities included typing,
filing, answering telephone,
scheduling appointments.

℘ 外國公司內總務部經理的
祕書。職責包括打字、整
理檔案，接電話、安排約
會。

㈦ 特殊才能

℘ Experienced operator：Word
Processor SV 68, 60wpm.

℘ 有經驗的操作人員：文字處
理機SV68型，每分鐘60字。

℘ Multilingual：Fluency in spoken
and written English. Competency in spoken Spanish.

℘ 通多種語言：英語說寫流
利。善於講西班牙文。

℘ Office skills include：operating
English wordprocessor and
personal computer, taking
shorthand 80 wpm.

℘ 辦公室工作技能包括：操
作英文文字處理機及個人
電腦、速記每分鐘80字。

℘ Working knowledge of all
common office machines.

℘ 對所有的一般辦公室用機
器有應用知識。

** schedule〔ˈskɛdʒʊl〕*v.* 排定；安排
multilingual〔ˌmʌltɪˈlɪŋgwəl〕*adj.* 通曉多種語言的

(八) 個人資質的表達

ℰ Ability to organize, coordinate and supervise work.

ℰ 具組織、協調及督責工作的能力。

ℰ Ability to listen and sensitivity to the needs of others

ℰ 能傾聽,對別人的需求敏感。

ℰ Adaptable, versatile, able to apportion time, industrious.

ℰ 能適應狀況,變通,分配時間,勤勉不懈。

ℰ Attentive to detail. Prepared accurate and timely reports.

ℰ 留心細節。準備準確而適時的報告。

ℰ Comprehension of financial statements.

ℰ 能理解財務報告。

ℰ Developed ability to work well with others.

ℰ 和別人合作能勝任愉快。

ℰ Developed communication and public relations skills.

ℰ 溝通佳、具公關技巧。

ℰ Enjoy working with people. Responsible, dependable.

ℰ 喜歡和別人一同工作。負責可靠。

** coordinate〔koˊɔrdṇ,et〕v. 協調　supervise〔,supəˊvaɪz〕v. 監督
versatile〔ˊvɝsətɪl〕adj. 會變通的　apportion〔əˊpɔrʃən〕v. 分派;分配
financial〔faɪˊnænʃəl〕adj. 財務的;金融的
comprehension〔,kɑmprɪˊhɛnʃən〕n. 理解;了解

ʊ Highly motivated and a team participant.

ʊ 企圖心很強，小組參與者。

ʊ Like to be challenged with a responsible job.

ʊ 喜歡迎戰責任重大的工作。

ʊ Like to take on new challenges and responsibilities.

ʊ 希望承擔新的挑戰及責任。

ʊ Maintain good human relations.

ʊ 維繫良好的人際關係。

❋❋ ─────────────────────

- **active**〔ˈæktɪv〕*adj.* 主動活躍的
- **aggressive**〔əˈgrɛsɪv〕*adj.* 積極有衝勁的
- **alert**〔əˈlɜt〕*adj.* 機敏靈活的
- **ambitious**〔æmˈbɪʃəs〕*adj.* 滿懷雄心的
- **analytical**〔ˌænɭˈɪtɪkɭ〕*adj.* 善於分析的
- **capable**〔ˈkepəbɭ〕*adj.* 幹練的
- **competent**〔ˈkɑmpətənt〕*adj.* 勝任愉快的
- **conscientious**〔ˌkɑnʃɪˈɛnʃəs〕*adj.* 謹慎盡責的

❋❋ ─────────────────────

- **constructive**〔kənˈstrʌktɪv〕*adj.* 建設性的
- **creative**〔krɪˈetɪv〕*adj.* 富創造力的
- **dedicated**〔ˈdɛdəˌketɪd〕*adj.* 具奉獻精神的；專注的
- **dependable**〔dɪˈpɛndəbɭ〕*adj.* 十分可靠的
- **disciplined**〔ˈdɪsəplɪnd〕*adj.* 有紀律的
- **discrete**〔dɪˈskrit〕*adj.* 分立的
- **dynamic**〔daɪˈnæmɪk〕*adj.* 精悍的
- **efficient**〔əˈfɪʃənt〕*adj.* 有效率的

- **energetic** 〔 ˌɛnɚˈdʒɛtɪk 〕 *adj.* 精力充沛的
- **enthusiastic** 〔 ɪnˌθjuzɪˈæstɪk 〕 *adj.* 充滿熱誠的
- **forceful** 〔 ˈforsfəl 〕 *adj.* 效果強烈的
- **ingenious** 〔 ɪnˈdʒinjəs 〕 *adj.* 聰明靈巧的
- **inventive** 〔 ɪnˈvɛntɪv 〕 *adj.* 獨創的
- **logical** 〔 ˈlɑdʒɪkl̩ 〕 *adj.* 條理分明的
- **loyal** 〔 ˈlɔɪəl 〕 *adj.* 忠誠不貳的
- **methodical** 〔 məˈθɑdɪkl̩ 〕 *adj.* 秩序井然的

※※————————————————

- **motivated** 〔 ˈmotəˌvetɪd 〕 *adj.* 有爆發力的
- **objective** 〔 əbˈdʒɛktɪv 〕 *adj.* 客觀的
- **practical** 〔 ˈpræktɪkl̩ 〕 *adj.* 實際的
- **realistic** 〔 ˌriəˈlɪstɪk 〕 *adj.* 實事求是的
- **reliable** 〔 rɪˈlaɪəbl̩ 〕 *adj.* 可以信賴的
- **responsible** 〔 rɪˈspɑnsəbl̩ 〕 *adj.* 負責盡職的
- **sincere** 〔 sɪnˈsɪr 〕 *adj.* 誠懇真摯的
- **systematic** 〔 ˌsɪstəˈmætɪk 〕 *adj.* 有系統的

第四篇

英文履歷表
範　例

The Resume

<u>RESUME</u>

2nd Fl., 24,
Yung-kang st.,   <u>FANNY CHAN</u>
Taipei 10623
(02) 396-5248

Born: June 12, 1987
5'1" 108 lbs; Single
Excellent Health

<u>OBJECTIVE</u>

To obtain an entry-level secretarial position which offers
development opportunity for a career as administrative
secretary.

<u>EDUCATION</u>

2005-present   Secretarial Course, Ming Chuan University
                Coursework include: secretarial principles,
                office administration, management, computer
                programming, business English, accounting,
                bookkeeping.
2002-2005   Chung Cheng High School, Taipei.

<u>EXPERIENCE</u>

2005-present   Clerk at Taian Co., Taipei. Full-time in
                summers, part-time during semesters. Perform
                general office administration assignments.
                Supervisors praise my efficiency and
                productivity.

<u>SKILLS</u>

Abacus Caculation 2nd class, 1997
Typing 50wpm

<u>ACTIVITIES</u>

Captain of volleyball team, Ming Chuan University

<u>PERSONAL QUALITIES</u>

Communication skills, accuracy in handling details,
cheerful personality, strong leadership, and a sense of
responsibility.

REFERENCES   Will be furnished upon request.

英文履歷表英漢對照

履 歷 表

詹 芬 妮

台北市10623永康街
24號2樓
（02）396-5248

生日：1987年6月12日
5呎1吋，108磅；未婚
健康情形極佳

希望之職務

得到初級祕書的職位，提供行政祕書職業的發展機會。

學　　歷

2005年至今　　　祕書課程；銘傳大學
　　　　　　　　課程包括：祕書原理，辦公室行政，管理學，
　　　　　　　　電腦程式設計，商用英文，會計，簿記。

2002年到2005年　台北中正高中

經　　歷

2005年至今　　　台北台安公司辦事員。暑假時專任，學期中兼差。
　　　　　　　　執行一般辦公室行政的分派工作。管理者讚賞我的
　　　　　　　　效率及生產力。

技　　能

珠算二級，1997年。打字每分鐘50個字

活　　動

銘傳大學排球隊隊長

個人特質

溝通技巧，處理細節精確，個性開朗，領導力強，有責任感。

保證人　　　如有要求將會提出

The Resume

Qualifications of Hsiao-ch'i Chou

161, Lane 191,
King-shan S. Rd., Sec. 2,   (02) 281-1882
Taipei, 10722

Position applied for: Executive Assistant

EXPERIENCE

2007-Present   Administrative assistant to the President
                of Feinberg Corporation. Responsibilities
                include:
                1. Typing memorandums and reports, receiving
                   visitors, answering telephone, arranging
                   appointments.
                2. Writing letters and reports for the
                   President's signature.

2005-2007   Administrative assistant to Sales Manager
                of Peabody Co., Ltd. Responsibilities
                included:
                1. Helping develop daily work schedule.
                2. Assisting customers on telephone or in
                   person.

2003-2005   Secretary-typist, Apex Trading Co., Ltd.,
                Taipei.
                Typed letters, contracts, shipping
                documents.

2001-2003   Sales clerk at Daily Stores (full time
                during school vacations and part-time
                during semesters).
                Waited on customers, assisted with typing
                and filing.

** administrative 〔əd'mɪnə,stretɪv〕 *adj.* 管理的；行政的

英文履歷表英漢對照

周曉琪 所備資格

台北市 10722 金山南路
二段 191 巷 161 號

（02）281-1882

應徵工作職位：行政助理

經　　　歷

2007 年至今　　　　　芬柏格公司董事長行政助理。職責包括：
　　　　　　　　　　　1. 備忘錄及報告打字。接待訪客，回電話、安排
　　　　　　　　　　　　約會。
　　　　　　　　　　　2. 書寫信件及報告讓董事長簽字。

2005 年至 2007 年　　皮巴帝有限公司銷售經理之行政助理。職責包括：
　　　　　　　　　　　1. 協助每日工作進度。
　　　　　　　　　　　2. 以電話或親自幫助顧客。

2003 年至 2005 年　　台北阿帕士貿易有限公司之祕書兼打字員。
　　　　　　　　　　　信件、合同、裝船文件打字。

2001 年至 2003 年　　每日商店銷售店員（學校長假時專任，學期中兼
　　　　　　　　　　　差。）服務顧客，協助打字及建檔。

EDUCATION

2001-2003 Taipei College of Business.
Courses completed:
secretarial procedures, accounting,
bookkeeping, data processing, typewriting,
wordprocessing, business English.

1998-2001 Tainan Commercial Vocational
Senior High School.

SKILLS Typing 60wpm.

PERSONAL DATA Born: July 15, 1979 5'2", 110 lbs.
Single Excellent Health

REFERENCES AND FURTHER DETAILS TO BE FURNISHED UPON
REQUEST

【標題參考】：

◇ **OBJECTIVE:** Management position in accounting
with opportunities for further
advancement.

◇ **JOB OBJECTIVE:** Entry-level position in computer
programming. Eventual goal is to
become a systems analyst.

◇ **POSITION APPLIED FOR:** A position in the sales department,
preferably on the managerial-level.

◇ **EMPLOYMENT OBJECTIVE:** Entry-level position in marketing
with the possibility of moving into
management.

◇ **POSITION SOUGHT:** A reporter in foreign affairs,
ultimate goal is to become an
editor.

學　　　　歷

2001年至2003年　　台北商業技術學院，修完課程：

祕書程序、會計、簿記、資料處理、打字、文字處理、商用英文。

1998年至2001年　　台南高商

技　　　　能　　打字每分鐘 60 個字

個 人 資 料　　生日： 1979 年 7 月 15 日　　　5 呎 2 吋，110 磅

未婚　　　　　　　　　健康情形極佳

保證人及更詳細資料如有要求將會提出。

【要點說明】：書寫自己應徵的職務時，標題可有下列變化，內容方面也可詳盡道出自己所追求的目標。

目　　　標：　會計方面的管理職務，有陞遷的機會。

工 作 目 標：　電腦程式設計的初等職位。最終目標在於成為系統分析師。

申 請 職 位：　行銷部門的職務，在管理階層尤佳。

工 作 目 標：　市場交易的初等職位，有進入管理職務的可能性。

謀 求 職 位：　外國事務的記者，最終目標在成為編輯。

The Resume

Milly Yeh

3rd Fl., 142, Chang-an E. Rd., Sec. 2, Taipei 10629	Born June 13, 1978 5'2" 105 lbs; Married Excellent health

OBJECTIVE: To serve as executive secretary to a hard-working executive of an American-affiliated company who needs an assistant with enterprise and capacity.

QUALIFICATIONS: Experience as secretary for ten years, six of these with top executives of a foreign-affiliated company.

EXPERIENCE: Administrative assistant and executive secretary, Stanford Ltd. Taipei.

2007–
Present
Served as administrative assistant to president; set up all executive staff meetings, prepared agenda and minutes; assisted in preparation of letters and reports, prepared routine correspondence for signature of president. Maintained his office in his absence.

2004-2007
Executive secretary to executive vice president.
Assisted in his administrative duties; arranged meetings and trips; wrote routine letters and reports.

2001-2004
Secretary to vice president in charge of marketing.
Served him by arranging trips, writing correspondence, and typing sales reports.

** executive〔ɪgˊzɛkjutɪv〕 *adj.* 執行的　*n.* 經理主管級人員

英文履歷表英漢對照

葉　蜜　莉

台北市 10629 長安東路
二段 142 號 3 樓

生日：1978 年 6 月 13 日
　5 呎 2 吋，105 磅，已婚
健康情形極佳

目　　標： 擔任美商公司中勤奮工作高級主管的執行祕書，高級主管所需助理是有進取心並且能幹。

資　　格： 祕書經驗十年，其中六年是外商公司高級主管的祕書。

經　　歷： 台北史丹佛有限公司行政助理暨執行祕書。

2007 年
至今

擔任董事長行政助理；安排所有高級主管人員會議，準備議程及會議記錄；協助信件報告之準備，準備給董事長簽名的例行連繫。董事長不在時，繼續辦公室之事。

2004 年
至 2007 年

執行副董事長之執行祕書。
協助行政任務；安排會議及旅行；書寫例行信件報告。

2001 年
至 2004 年

負責市場交易的副總經理祕書。
安排行程，書寫連繫信件，打銷售報告的字。

EDUCATION:

1999-2000   Intermediate and advanced executive secre-
              tarial courses of Shih Chien University
              (Correspondence course).

1997-2001   English Department, Fu Jen Catholic
              University.

SKILLS: Typewriting 60 wpm, Shorthand 90 wpm.

REFERENCES: To be furnished upon request.

【 學歷格式暨內容 】：

2005-2008   Department of Business Management.
              Tamkang University.
              Special Training: Accounting, Economics,
              Office Management, International Trade,
              Marketing & Finance, Statistics,
              Business Law, Labor Law, Management
              Problems, Business English,
              Activities: worked in a 2-week social
                          project and planned the whole
                          schedule

2000-2005   Taipei College of Business.
              Major: Business Management.

** intermediate〔,ɪntɚˈmidɪɪt〕 *adj.* 中間的；中級的
   shorthand〔ˈʃɔrt,hænd〕 *n.* 速記

學　歷：

1999年	實踐大學中級及高級執行祕書課程。
至2000年	（函授課程）
1997年	輔仁大學
至2001年	英文系

技　能： 打字每分鐘60個字，速記每分鐘90字。

保證人： 如有需要將會補充。

【要點提示】：在書寫學歷時，除了寫出專業訓練的科目外，亦可補充
　　　　　　　比較特殊的活動項目。

2005年至2008年　企業管理學系。

淡江大學。

特別的訓練：會計、經濟、辦公室管理、國際貿易、
市場及財務、統計、商業法、勞工法、管理問題、
商用英文。

活動：從事兩週的社會計劃，並作出整個的時間表。

2000年至2005年　台北商業技術學院。

主修：企業管理。

The Resume

DAR-TIAN HONG

2F, 85 Chung Shan N. Rd., Sec. 2   Born: November 4, 1986
Taipei 10413   5' 8" 145 lbs; Single
(02) 3964885   Excellent Health

OBJECTIVE

To obtain an entry-level position in an investment firm, with prospects of moving up to higher positions with acquisition of more experience.

EDUCATION

2004-2008   Department of Mass Communication, bachelor of arts, Soochow University.
              Courses completed: Comparative literature, Linguistics, Rhetorical theory, Visual communication, Organizational and speech communication, Mass communication research, Propaganda, Public opinion, Monetary policy, General Economic theory.
2000-2004   Kaohsiung High School.

EXPERIENCE

7/06-9/06   Tour guide during the summer vacation for Pacific Travel Agency Inc. Generally conducted tours for foreign tourists on trip around the city and immediate environs.

SKILLS

Familiar with use of a word processor

ACTIVITIES

Club president for Kaohsiung High School Glee Club.

** propaganda〔,prɑpə'gændə〕*n.* 宣傳   environs〔ɪn'vaɪrənz〕*n.* 郊外；近郊

英文履歷表英漢對照

洪　達　天

台北市 10413 中山北路
二段 85 號 2 樓
（02）3964885

生日：1986 年 11 月 4 日
　5 呎 8 吋，145 磅；未婚
健康情形極佳

目　　　標

在一家投資公司獲得初級職位，隨著獲得越多的經驗，有進昇更高職位的遠景。

學　　　歷

2004 年至 2008 年　　　東吳大學大眾傳播學士
　　　　　　　　　　　　修畢課程：比較文學、語言語、修辭理論、視
　　　　　　　　　　　　學溝通、組織及演說溝通、大眾傳播研究、宣
　　　　　　　　　　　　傳、興論、貨幣政策、一般經濟理論。

2000 年至 2004 年　　　高雄中學

經　　　歷

06 年 7 月至 06 年 9 月　　暑假期間爲太平洋旅遊代辦公司觀光導遊。爲
　　　　　　　　　　　　外國的觀光客旅行時在城區及最近的郊外作一
　　　　　　　　　　　　般的嚮導旅行。

技　　　能

熟悉文字處理機的使用。

活　　　動

高雄中學合唱團團長。

PERSONAL QUALITIES

Enthusiasm. Ability to solve problems creatively. Strong interpersonal skills. Ability to work as a member of a team. Persuasive. Sensitive to current trends and issues.

REFERENCES: Will be furnished upon request.

【標題參考】：

■ **OCCUPATIONAL HISTORY:**

2005 - present	editor, Sinorama Magazine.
2003 - 2005	reporter, China Post.

■ **WORK HISTORY:**

2004 - present	secretary, China Export LTD.
2000 - 2004	typist, Central Exporters.

■ **PROFESSIONAL HISTORY:**

Wang Laboratories Boston, Massachusetts, USA January 2002-March 2007	Systems analyst.
Multitech Computers Taipei, Taiwan, R.O.C. January 2000-November 2001	Computer programmer

■ **EMPLOYMENT:**

2000 - 2002	Loan officer, City Bank of Taipei. Developed a customer credit rating process which has become standard at City Bank.
1995 - 2000	Teller, Land Bank of Taipei. Devised a system to clear checks in half the usual time.

<u>個 人 特 質</u>

熱心，能具創意的解決問題，人際關係技巧強，能成為小組工作的一員，具有說服力，對現今的趨勢及問題很敏感。

<u>保證人</u>：如有需求將可補充。

【**要點提示**】：在寫經歷時，標題除了 Experience, Work Experience 外，也有下列變化。

工作經歷：	2005 年至今	編輯，光華雜誌。
	2003 年至 2005 年	記者，英文中國郵報。
工作經歷：	2004 年至今	祕書，中華出口有限公司。
	2000 年至 2004 年	打字員，中央出口公司。

職業經歷：王氏研究室　　　　　　系統分析師
　　　　　美國麻州波士頓
　　　　　2002 年 1 月至 2007 年 3 月

　　　　　多科技電腦公司　　　　　電腦程式設計師
　　　　　中華民國台灣台北
　　　　　2000 年 1 月至 2001 年 11 月

工　　作：2000 年至 2002 年　借貸部職員，台北市銀行。
　　　　　　　　　　　　　　　發展客戶的信用估計程序，已成為銀行中標準。
　　　　　1995 年至 2000 年　出納員，台北土地銀行。
　　　　　　　　　　　　　　　設計出只要平常一半時間就可交換清算支票的系統。

The Resume

56, Lane 47,
Chu-lin Rd., Yung-ho,   (02) 9246279
Taipei County 20237

RESUME
Maureen Shao

PERSONAL DATA
Born 5/12/85   Single   Excellent health

OBJECTIVE
To serve an American-affiliated firm as a junior
accountant.

QUALIFICATIONS
University education in accounting, involving use of
computers.

EDUCATION
2004-2008 Department of Commerce, National Taiwan
          University.
          Major: Accounting
                  Courses included: principles of account-
                  ing, fundamentals of bookkeeping, cost
                  accounting, financial statements
                  analysis, financial management, EDP
                  accounting.
          Minors: Information Science
                  Courses included: introduction to data-
                  processing, programming theories,
                  programming exercises, introduction to
                  information sciences.
2001-2004 Hsinchu Girls' High School.

** fundamental 〔 ,fʌndə'mɛntl 〕*n.* 基本原理

英文履歷表英漢對照

台北縣 20237 永和市
竹林路 47 巷 56 號

（02）9246279

履　歷　表
邵　穆　琳

個　人　資　料

生日：1985 年 5 月 12 日　　　未　婚　　　　　健康情形極佳

目　　標

擔任美商公司的中級會計。

資　　格

大學會計方會的訓練，包括電腦的使用。

學　　歷

2004 年－ 2008 年　　國立台灣大學商學系
主修：會計
課程包括：會計學原理、簿記基本原理、成本會計、決算分析、財務管理、電子資料處理會計。
副修：資訊科學
課程包括：資料處理導論、程式設計原理、程式設計練習、資訊科學導論。

2001 年－ 2004 年　　新竹女中

EXTRACURRICULAR ACTIVITIES

President of Accounting Study Club, National Taiwan University, 2007.
Organized an exhibit of its study report a University Festival, 2007.

AWARD AND HONORS

Scholarship from Culture Foundation, 2007.

SUMMER JOB

Clerked at Accounting Department of Sunshine Supermarket, 2006 and 2007.

QUALIFICATION CERTIFICATES

Examination of Data-processing Technicians, Programmer, 2007.

REFERENCES: Will be furnished upon request.

【結論範例】：

The field of biology fascinates me. In college I majored in biology and was a member of the Biology Club. I also have practical experience working in the laboratory doing blood and urine analyses. I seek a position that will allow me to continue my interest in biology.

課 外 活 動

2007 年，國立台灣大學會計研習社社長。

2007 年，校慶時策畫研習報告展。

獎 賞 及 榮 譽

2007 年，文化基金會獎學金。

暑 期 工 讀

2006 年及 2007 年，陽光超級市場會計部門職員。

資 格 檢 定

2007 年，資料處理技能考試，程式設計人員。

保證人：如有需要將會提出

【要點說明】：在履歷表末尾提出結論時，針對自己所特長的地方強調，
　　　　　　　將大大增進獲得面試的機會，標題可採用 *Summary*，
　　　　　　　Conclusion，*In Conclusion*。

　　生物的領域使我非常入迷。大學時我主修生物，是生物社的社員。
同時有在實驗室裏作血液和尿液分析的實際工作經驗。我謀求一個能讓
我持續生物方面興趣的工作。

The Resume

RESUME

IVY CHUANG
Age 29 (March 20, 1981)
Single, Excellent Health

3rd Fl., 17,
Ho-ping E. Rd., Sec. 2
Taipei 10311
(02) 5413723

OBJECTIVE

Position in Accounting Department leading to a position
in management.

QUALIFICATIONS

Good university education combined with practical
experience in accounting and familiality with Western
style accounting.

EMPLOYMENT

2002-present ('08-present)	Dafa Trading Co., Ltd., Taipei. Corporate Accounting Section, Taipei Head Office. Gained experience in consolidating accounts of overseas affiliates and subsidiaries. Prepared detailed financial records including current and historical reports.
('05-'08)	Accounting Department, Dafa Trading (USA), Inc., N.Y. Gained practical experience in American style accounting and working with American staff.
('02-'05)	Machinery Accounting Section, Taipei Head Office. Performed routine book-keeping and basic accounting tasks including journal entries and report preparation.

** consolidate〔kən'salə,det〕*v.* 鞏固；強化

subsidiary〔səb'sɪdɪ,ɛrɪ〕*n.* 附屬公司

英文履歷表英漢對照

履　歷　表

莊愛薇
29 歲（1981 年 3 月 20 日生）
未婚，健康情形極佳

台北市 10311 和平東路
二段 17 號 3 樓
（02）5413723

目　　　標

會計部門的職位步向管理的職位

資　　　格

優良的大學教育加上會計方面實務經驗以及熟悉西式會計。

工　　　作

2002 年至今 （08 年至今）	台北大發貿易有限公司 台北總公司，共同會計部門。 強化海外分部及附屬公司會計方面得到經驗。 準備詳細的財務記錄，包括當今及歷史性的報告。
（05年至08年）	美國紐約大發公司會計部門。 在美式會計方面得到實務經驗，以及和美國工作人員一同工作。
（02年至05年）	台北總公司機械會計部門。 執行例行簿記以及基本會計工作，包括日誌記載和準備報告。

EDUCATION

1998–2002	Department of Accounting, National Chengchi University. Major: Accounting-- accounting principles, management accounting, EDP accounting, corporate finance.
1995–1998	Kaohsiung Girls' High School.

EXTRACURRICULAR ACTIVITIES

Treasurer, Student Council, National Chengchi University.

SKILLS   Computer language: Cobol.

REFERENCES Will be supplied on request.

【 學歷格式暨內容 】：

Department of Agricultural Economics, National Taiwan University, 2004–2008.

Curriculum: 1) Farm & Ranch Management

2) Agricultural Prices

3) International Trade

4) Agricultural Economics

5) Land Economics

6) Accounting

7) Statistics

8) Quantitative Analysis

9) Speech and Technical Writing

10) Business Management

學　　　　歷
　　1998 年　　　　國立政治大學會計系
　　至 2002 年　　　主修：會計……會計學原理，經營會計
　　　　　　　　　　　　　電子資料處理會計，共同財務學。
1995年至1998年　　高雄女中

課 外 活 動
國立政治大學學生委員會財務。

技　　　　能　　　電腦語言：Cobol

保　證　人　　　　如有需求將會提出

【要點提示】：履歷表的書寫格式沒有標準，此種寫出課程內容的適合
　　　　　　　　甫出校門的畢業生，表示出自己的資格與能力。

農業經濟學系，國立台灣大學， 2004 年至 2008 年。

課　　程：　　1）　農場及果園管理
　　　　　　　2）　農業物價
　　　　　　　3）　國際貿易
　　　　　　　4）　農業經濟學
　　　　　　　5）　土地經濟學
　　　　　　　6）　會　　計
　　　　　　　7）　統 計 學
　　　　　　　8）　定量分析
　　　　　　　9）　演講與專題寫作
　　　　　　10）　企業管理

The Resume

MARIE CHAO

59 Sinyi Road, Sec. 2,
Taipei 10253
Telephone: (02) 7025800

OBJECTIVE:　　　Business Assistant

PERSONAL:　　　Birthdate: October 1, 1986　　Single
　　　　　　　　160cm　　　50kg　　　Excellent health

EDUCATION:　　　2003-2008　　B.A. Degree in Business
　　　　　　　　　　　　　　　Administration
　　　　　　　　　　　　　　　Major: International Business
　　　　　　　　　　　　　　　National Chung Hsing Univer-
　　　　　　　　　　　　　　　sity
　　　　　　　　2000-2003　　Chiayi Girls' High School.

EDUCATIONAL
HIGHLIGHTS:　　Principles of　　　　Business Economies
　　　　　　　　　　Accounting　　　　Statistics
　　　　　　　　Banking Laws　　　　Corporate Finance
　　　　　　　　Financial Markets　　Personnel Admin-
　　　　　　　　Management Science　　　istration
　　　　　　　　Money Management　　　Organization
　　　　　　　　Human Resources　　　　Behaviour
　　　　　　　　　Management

STUDENT
ACTIVITIES:　　Honors Society, Chung Hsing University
　　　　　　　　Student council President, Chung Hsing
　　　　　　　　University, 2006
　　　　　　　　Campus Ministry

SUMMER JOBS:

Summer of 2005　　Leopard Shoes Co., Ltd.　　Filing Clerk
　　　　　　　　95, Keelung Rd., Sec. 1.
　　　　　　　　Taipei

英文履歷表英漢對照

趙　美　莉

台北市 10253
信義路二段 59 號
電話：（02）7025800

目　　　標： 業務助理

個　　　人： 生日：1986 年 10 月 1 日　　　未婚
160 公分　　　　50 公斤　　　健康情形極佳

學　　　歷： 2003 年至 2008 年　　企業管理學士學位
主修：國際貿易
國立中興大學

2000 年至 2003 年　　嘉義女中

課程精采部分： 會計原理　　　　商業經濟
銀行法　　　　　統計
財務市場　　　　合作經濟
管理學　　　　　人事管理
財務管理　　　　行為科學
人力資源管理

學 生 活 動： 中興大學榮譽學會
2006 年中興大學學生會主席
校園內閣

暑 期 工 讀： 豹鞋業公司　　　檔案處理員
2005 年夏天　　　台北市基隆路一段 95 號

REFERENCES: References are furnished on request.

INTERESTS: Like listening to pop music. Go dancing
                   on the weekends. Occasionally do some
                   sculpture with clay.

【 學歷格式暨內容 】：

2004 - 2008   National Chung Hsing University
               Taichung
               B. Sc., 2008
               Majored in Botany
                 Scholastic Average: 82
               Minored in Horticulture
                 Scholastic Average: 84
               Scholarships:
               2005: Retired Serviceman's Dependent
                     Scholarship
               2006: Scholarship from Council for Agricul-
                     tural Planning and Development
               2008: Scholarship from President of the
                     University

2001 - 2004   Changhwa High School.

保　證　人：　保證人如有需求將補充。

興　　　趣：　喜歡聽流行音樂，週末時跳舞，
　　　　　　　偶而用黏土作雕塑。

【要點提示】：對才自學校畢業的人而言，優良的成績是對自己勤奮及
　　　　　　　才智一項有力的證明，列出優秀的成績及所領過的獎學
　　　　　　　金，會使履歷表更具可看性。

2004 年至 2008 年　　國立中興大學
　　　　　　　　　　台中市
　　　　　　　　　　理學士，2008 年
　　　　　　　　　　主修植物學
　　　　　　　　　　　學業平均：82 分
　　　　　　　　　　副修園藝
　　　　　　　　　　　學業平均：84 分
　　　　　　　　　　獎學金：
　　　　　　　　　　2005 年：榮民子女獎學金
　　　　　　　　　　2006 年：農業發展委員會獎學金
　　　　　　　　　　2008 年：大學校長獎學金

2001 年至 2004 年　　彰化高中

The Resume

Jaan-chuan Lee
49 5F Lane 37,
Keelung Rd.,Sec. 2,
Taipei 10264
(02) 700-2549

OBJECTIVE: ASSISTANT MERCHANDISER FOR A DEPT. STORE

WORK COVERED: Planned and did actual purchases of merchandise from manufacturers and distributors for resale in chain store worked for. Knowledge of men's line of fashion. Research on customer preferences. Testing of the salability of products. Did recommendations on analysis and findings of research to senior management officials. Establish extensive contacts and did negotiations with manufacturers and distributors.

Handled a variety of accounts as assistant merchandiser of chain store worked for. Succeeded in raising yearly sales volume by 20% at profit margins of from 50-100%. Department worked for handled annual sales volume of between NT$10 and 15 million.

MANAGEMENT
EXPERIENCE: Managed sales staff for nationwide operations. Developed ways of making more efficient the promotion, delivery, stocking and purchasing of goods. Helped set up chain store branches for firm. Managed the direction and planning of research members.

** manufacturer〔͵mænjə'fæktʃərə〕*n.* 製造商

distributor〔dɪ'strɪbjətə〕*n.* 經銷商　***chain store*** 連鎖商店

line〔laɪn〕*n.* 商品的一種　margin〔'mɑrdʒɪn〕*n.* 盈餘；利潤

volume〔'vɑljəm〕*n.* 數量；總額

英文履歷表英漢對照

李　展　川
台北市 10264 基隆路二段
37 巷 49 號 5 樓
（02）700-2549

目　　　標：　百貨公司的採購助理

工 作 涵 蓋：　計劃並實際向製造廠商和經銷商購買產品，在所工
作的連鎖店再賣出。男士流行商品的知識，研究顧
客的喜好。試驗產品的銷售可能性。
在研究的分析和發現上，對高級管理人員作建議。
和製造廠商和經銷商建立廣泛的接觸，並作交涉談判。
在連鎖店工作作採購助理時，處理各種不同的帳目。
成功地提高年度銷售量百分之二十，利潤盈餘由百
分之五十到百分之百。在所工作的部門處理每年的
銷售量在一千萬到一千五百萬之間。

管 理 經 驗：　管理行銷人員全國性的工作。發展推廣、遞送、貯
存購買貨品更有效率的方法。協助公司設立連鎖分
店。管理研究人員的方向及計劃。

PROSPECT
RESEARCH:　　Started study on developing new lines of
　　　　　　　men's fashion wear cooperating with fashion
　　　　　　　designers and market researchers. Present
　　　　　　　final reports detailing findings and
　　　　　　　recommendations.

PERSONAL
SOLICITATION:　Manufacturers and Distributors for men's
　　　　　　　line of goods.

FIRMS:

2005 – 2008　　Oriental Chain Stores Ltd.
　　　　　　　Assistant Merchandiser

2003 – 2005　　John Class Sportswear Co.
　　　　　　　Sales Representative

2002 – 2003　　Fiorucci Specialty Boutique
　　　　　　　Sales Clerk

EDUCATION:　　Soochow University: B.S. Marketing

【 工作職務說明 】：

　　Responsible for the day-to-day operations of hotel
dining service. Supervised the purchasing, preparation,
presentation of food, and the training of the dining room
wait staff. Worked in close cooperation with hotel
management to determine trends in customer tastes and to
implement the necessary changes.

　　** boutique〔bu'tik〕*n.* 精品店；銷售最新流行服飾的小商店
　　B.S. 理學士（ = *Bachelor of Science* ）

希望作的研究：　　和流行設計師及市場研究者合作，開始研究發展新
　　　　　　　　　的一種男士流行服飾。提出詳細說明的發現以及建
　　　　　　　　　議的最後報告。

個 人 客 戶：　　男士貨品的製造廠商和經銷商。

公　　　　司：

2005 年至 2008 年　　東方連鎖店有限公司　採購助理

2003 年至 2005 年　　約翰克雷斯運動服飾公司　銷售代表

2002 年至 2003 年　　菲歐路西特產品流行名店　銷售店員

學　　　　歷：　　東吳大學：市場學理學士

【要點提示】：Functional Resume 是將工作性質相似的集中説明，
　　　　　　　好讓雇主明白你的能力所在。

　　負責處理旅舘每日的進餐服務。督導採買所需準備的東西，弄好食
物，餐廳服務人員的訓練。與旅舘管理部門密切合作，決定顧客愛好的
趨向以及執行必要的改變。

The Resume

<u>HO-CHUNG CHAN</u>

4F, 45 Wen Chou St.,
Taipei 10253
(02) 3217359

Born April 15, 1984
5' 4" 120lbs; Married
Excellent health

<u>OBJECTIVE</u>:

To serve as a Marketing Assistant in a Multinational Corporation with a view to promotion in position and assignment in parent company's branch abroad.

<u>QUALIFICATIONS</u>:

Has worked for a multinational firm for two years and in the marketing department of a local department store for 1 year.

<u>EXPERIENCE</u>:

2008-
Present

Executive Promotions Manager Assistant for Rockwelle Industrial Concerns Inc. Work involves analysis of actual field studies to the reactions of potential purchasers of the company's products. Included also are planning and carrying out of research on consumer's preferences. Surveys conducted by telephone, mail or face-to-face questioning.

2007-2008

Sales manager assistant in Hsin Kuang Department Store.
Responsibilities include presentation of products in the Men's Section of the department store and training of sales force in the area.

** ***parent company*** （商）母公司（因擁有較多股份或因董事會的結構而控制另一公司者）

英文履歷表英漢對照

張 和 忠

台北市 10253
溫州街 45 號 4 樓
（02）3217359

生於 1984 年 4 月 15 日
5 呎 4 吋，120 磅，已婚
健康情形極佳

目 標： 在一家多國合作有限公司擔任市場銷售助理，在職位上有陞遷並能分派到海外母公司分部的展望。

資 格： 已在一家多國合資的公司工作兩年，並在當地百貨公司的市場部門待了一年。

經 歷：

2008 年至今　　洛克斐勒工業股份公司執行推廣經理助理
工作包括分析實際範圍的研究—直到可能購買公司產品者的反應。同時包括計劃和進行消費者喜好的研究。用電話、信件和面對面詢問來作考察。

2007 年至 2008 年　　新光百貨公司行銷經理助理
職責包括百貨公司內男士部門產品展示，訓練這範圍的銷售力量。

EDUCATION:

2003 - 2007	Bachelor's of Science degree in Business Administration with field of concentration on marketing. Courses taken: Marketing, Statistics, Accounting, Management, Finance. International Marketing and Distribution. International Economics. Ethics. Organizational Behaviour.
2000 - 2003	Cheng-Kung High School, Taipei.

SKILLS:　　　　Fluent in three languages: Mandarin, English, Japanese. Acquainted with computer uses for marketing.

FEFERENCES:　　To be furnished upon request.

【 工作職務說明 】：

　　Directed the development of instruction materials, the method of instruction, and the hiring of teachers to teach English as a second language. Have developed an English teaching program that has been widely praised by students for its innovation and effectiveness. As a result student enrollment have been increasing at a rate of 20 percent annually.

學　　　　　歷：

2003 年至 2007 年　　主修市場行銷的企業管理學士
　　　　　　　　　　　修過課程：市場學、統計學、會計、管理學、財
　　　　　　　　　　　政學、國際市場行銷及產銷分配、國際經濟、倫
　　　　　　　　　　　理學、組織行爲。

2000 年至 2003 年　　台北成功高中

技　　　　　能：　　三種語言流利：國語、英語、日語
　　　　　　　　　　熟悉市場行銷所用的電腦

保　　證　　人：　　如有需要將可提出。

【要點說明】：Functional Resume 除了將職務集中説明之外，列出
　　　　　　　工作上的成績，將讓雇主對你的能力留下深刻的印象。

　　管理教材的發展情形、教學方法、以及招聘教英文爲第二語言的老
師。已發展出英語教學計畫，其創新及效率廣爲學生讚賞。結果學生註
册每年以百分之二十的比例增加。

The Resume

59 3F Roosevelt Road, Sec. 3,
Taipei 10021   (02) 3415813

RESUME

HUEY-CHYI WANG

PERSONAL DATA

Born 8/10/87   Single   Excellent health

OBJECTIVE

To work in the International Sales Department of an
American-affiliated firm.

QUALIFICATIONS

University education in Business Administration with a
background in domestic sales promotion.

EDUCATION

2004 – 2008   Department of Business Administration, Sun
               Yat-sen University.
               Major: Business Administration
                       Courses included: International Finance,
                       Industrial Law, Organization and
                       Economics, Microeconomic Trade,
                       International Theory, Marketing,
                       Accounting, Management Science, Busi-
                       ness and Public Policy.
               Minors: Money Management
                       Courses included: Economics, Banking,
                       Finance, Taxation.

2001 – 2004   Taichung Girls' High School.

英文履歷表英漢對照

台北市 10021 羅斯福路
三段 59 號 3 樓

（02）3415813

履　歷　表

王　慧　琪

個　人　資　料

生於 1987 年 8 月 10 日　　　未　婚　　　健康情形極佳

目　　　標

在美商公司的國際行銷部門工作。

資　　　格

企業管理的大學學歷，並有國內行銷推廣的經歷。

學　　　歷

2004 年至 2008 年　中山大學企業管理學系
　　　　　　　　　　主修：企業管理
　　　　　　　　　　　　　課程包括：國際財務、工業法、組織與經濟、
　　　　　　　　　　　　　個體經濟學論、國際貿易、市場學、會計、
　　　　　　　　　　　　　管理學、商業與公共政策。
　　　　　　　　　　副修：財務管理
　　　　　　　　　　　　　課程包括：經濟學、銀行學、財務學、稅務學

2001年至 2004 年　台中女中

EXTRACURRICULAR ACTIVITIES

Vice-Chairman of Society of BA majors, Sun Yat-sen
University, 2006.
Organized a conference on "Psychology in Corporate
Business"

AWARD AND HONORS

Scholarship from Business Development Foundation, 2004
Dean's List, Second Honors, consecutively from 2004-2008,
Sun Yat-sen University.

SUMMER JOB

Executive Assistant to the President, Yitai Co., Ltd.,
2007.

REFERENCES: Will be furnished upon request

【 工作職務 】：

2000-2006   News Editor
             Fushing Radio Network
             Taipei

             Supervised a staff of 20 writers. Responsible
             for the hiring and training of the news
             writing staff. And also have the final re-
             sponsibility for the accuracy of the news
             reported by Fushing. During my stay here its
             listening audience rose by over 10 percent
             annually. The news reports were singled out as
             the major reason for the increase in
             listeners.

** *dean's list* 大學中成績優秀學生之名單

consecutive〔kən'sɛkjətɪv〕*adj.* 連續的

課 外 活 動

2006 年，中山大學企業管理學會副會長。

組織了以「合作貿易心理」為題的研討會。

獎　　　賞

2004 年，商業發展基金會獎學金。

2004 年至 2008 年連續名列中山大學成績優秀學生之名單，第二名。

暑 期 工 讀

2007 年，益台有限公司，董事長執行助理。

保　證　人　如有需要將可提出。

【要點說明】：職務及業績可以增加工作經歷這一項目的份量，對於工作經驗豐富的人是個無往不利的利器。

2000 年至 2006 年　　新聞編輯

復興無線電廣播網

台北

管理二十個寫作的職員。負責招收訓練新聞寫作人員，同時對復興電台播出新聞的正確性負有最後的責任。在我停留此處期間，聽眾每年增加超過百分之十。聽眾增加的主要原因是挑選了新聞的播報。

The Resume

RESUME of

6th Fl., 852,
Ming-sheng E. Rd.,
Taipei 10200

Molly Su

(02) 7622413
Born: May 1, 1979

OBJECTIVE

A position in Foreign Trade Department, with opportunities for advancement to management position in the department.

QUALIFICATIONS

Eight years working experience in a trading firm coupled with educational background specialized in foreign trade.

EXPERIENCE

2002-Present (2008-Present)	Far East Trading Co., Ltd. Import Section, Synthetic Textiles Department Handled import of synthetic piecegoods from Hong Kong, Korea, Japan. Increased sales 30 percent during the period. Made frequent business trips to these countries to negotiate with textile mills.
(2006-2008)	Export Section, Synthetic Textiles Department Assisted section chief in export of synthetic piecegoods to North America and Europe. Made business trips twice to North America and once to Europe for sales promotion.
(2004-2006)	Foreign Exchange Section, Finance Department Handled L/C, bills of exchange, forward exchange.
(2002-2004)	Export Section, Shipping Department Arranged shipments and made out shipping documents.

** synthetic〔sɪn'θɛtɪk〕*adj.* 合成的；人工製造的

英文履歷表英漢對照

履　歷　表

台北市 10200 民生東路　　　　蘇　茉　莉　　　　（02）7622413
852 號 6 樓　　　　　　　　　　　　　　　　　　生日：1979 年 5 月 1 日

目　　　標

外貿部門的職位，有機會能晉升到該部門的經理職位。

資　　　格

八年在貿易公司的工作經驗，加上外貿方面專門訓練背景。

經　　　歷

2002 年至今　　　　　遠東貿易有限公司
（ 2008 年至今）　　　合成紡織部門進口組
　　　　　　　　　　　管理從香港、韓國、日本人造布匹的進口事宜。在
　　　　　　　　　　　那期間增加 30％ 銷售額。經常出差到這些國家跟
　　　　　　　　　　　紡織廠商洽。

2006 年至 2008 年　　　合成紡織部門出口組
　　　　　　　　　　　協助組長出口人造布匹到北美及歐洲。
　　　　　　　　　　　為提高銷售量，兩次出差北美，一次出差歐洲。

2004 年至 2006 年　　　財務部門外滙兌換組
　　　　　　　　　　　管理信用狀、滙票、預售外滙。

2002 年至 2004 年　　　船運部門出口組
　　　　　　　　　　　安排船運，書寫裝船文件。

EDUCATION

1998-2002	Department of International Trade, Tung Hai University
	Courses taken: international marketing, foreign trade practice, English business communication, international business management, foreign exchange.
	Vice-captain of tennis team.
1995-1998	Chung Sheng Girls' High School, Taipei
	President of Student Council

REFERENCES AND OTHER DETAILS TO BE SUPPLIED UPON REQUEST

【 學歷格式暨內容 】：

Bachelor of Arts in English, September 2003 to June 2007.

Providence University, Taichung.

Minor: Business Administration.

* Assisted in Home for Unwed Mothers.

* Vice President of Student Council, 2005.

* Secretary of Department Society, 2004.

Graduate of Tainan Girls' High School, 2003.

* Varsity Basketball and Volleyball.

* Swimming Team.

* Class leader (2 years).

學　　歷

1998年至2002年　　東海大學國際貿易系
　　　　　　　　　　修過課程：國際市場、外貿實務、英語商務溝通、
　　　　　　　　　　國際商務管理、外滙滙兌
　　　　　　　　　　網球隊副隊長

1995年至1998年　　台北中山女高，學生委員會會長。

保證人及其它細節如有需求將可提出

【要點提示】：此種學歷的格式與內容強調所參與的學校活動，表現出
　　　　　　　　積極活躍的個性，適用於即將踏入社會的新鮮人。

英語文學士，2003年9月至2007年6月。
台中靜宜大學。
副修：企業管理。
＊協助未婚媽媽之家。
＊學生會副主席，2005年。
＊系學會祕書，2004年。

台南女中畢業，2003年。
＊籃球排球校隊。
＊游泳隊。
＊班長（2年）。

The Resume

Qualifications of BIH-YEU CHANG

8th Fl., 3 Hsin Hai Road, Sec. 3,
Taipei 10233

(02) 341-9768

Position applied for: Staff for Personnel Department

EXPERIENCE

5/07-9/07   Propsman for Taiwan Television Enterprise
                 Ltd.
                 Help coordinate and arrange stage sets for
                 programs.

EDUCATION

2004-2008   Department of Management, Taiwan University
                 BA Public Relations
                 Courses taken: Communication Theory.
                 Management. Administrative Services. Labor
                 Relations. Business Ethics. Organizational
                 Behaviour. Communications. Business Policy.

2000-2004   The First Girls' High School, Taipei.

SKILLS   Graphic Arts. Have had works exhibited in
                 an art gallery.

PERSONAL DATA   Born: September 12, 1987   5' 4"   120 lbs.
                 Single   Excellent Health

REFERENCES AND FURTHER DETAILS TO BE FURNISHED UPON
REQUEST

** *graphic arts* 平面藝術；書畫雕刻藝術

英文履歷表英漢對照

張碧瑜所備資格

台北市 10233 辛亥路三段　　　　　　　　　　（02）341-9768
3 號 8 樓

應徵職位：人事部門職員

經　　　歷：

07 年 5 月至 07 年 9 月　　台灣電視公司的道具人員。
　　　　　　　　　　　　　協助協調安排節目的舞台佈景。

學　　　歷

2004 年至 2008 年　　　　台灣大學管理學系，公共關係學士
　　　　　　　　　　　　　修過課程：溝通理論、管理學、行政服務、勞
　　　　　　　　　　　　　工關係、商業倫理學、組織行為、溝通學、商
　　　　　　　　　　　　　業政策。

2000 年至 2004 年　　　　台北一女中

技　　　能　　　　　　　　平面藝術。曾有作品在藝術畫廊展出。

個 人 資 料　　　　　　　生日：1987 年 9 月 12 日　　5 呎 4 吋，120 磅
　　　　　　　　　　　　　未婚　　　　　　　　　　　健康情形極佳

保證人和另外的細節如有需求將可提出

The Resume

Tessa Mo

2nd Fl., 38, Alley 12,   (02) 3416923
Lane 182, Roosevelt Rd., Sec. 3,   Born: July 7, 1977
Taipei 10319

OBJECTIVE   Responsible managerial position in
                   personnel.

QUALIFICATIONS   Work experience in personnel affairs in
                   foreign capital environment coupled with
                   educational background specialized in
                   personnel management.

EXPERIENCE

2004-Present   Assistant to Personnel Director, Taiwan
                   Hamilton Co. Responsibilities include
                   recruitment, training, and personnel
                   management. Conduct extensive interviews.
                   Assist in establishing policies and making
                   decisions in the area of manpower management.

2000-2004   Personnel Department, Hoover Far East Co.
                   Responsibilities included assisting
                   Personnel Manager in general personnel
                   matters. Wrote job specifications and
                   job classfications.

EDUCATION

1996-2000   Department of Public Administration,
                   National Taiwan University.
                   Major: Business Administration with
                            empahsis on personnel. Courses
                            completed include personnel
                            management, behavioral science,
                            organization theory, psychology,
                            labor law

** specification〔,spɛsəfə'keʃən〕 *n.* 詳述

英文履歷表英漢對照

莫　黛　莎

台北市 10319 羅斯福路三段　　　　　　（02）3416923
182 巷 12 弄 38 號 2 樓　　　　　　　　生日：1977 年 7 月 7 日

目　　標　　人事方面負責管理的職位

資　　格　　外資環境裏人事事務的工作經驗，加上人事管理方面
　　　　　　　　專門的訓練背景。

經　　歷

2004 年　　　　台灣漢明頓公司人事主任助理
　至今　　　　　職責包括吸收人員、訓練、人事管理。作過很多面試訪談。
　　　　　　　　協助製訂政策，在人力管理方面作決策。

2000 年　　　　胡佛遠東公司人事部門
至 2004 年　　　職責包括在一般人事事務上協助人事經理。
　　　　　　　　寫出工作詳細敘述及工作分類。

學　　歷

1996 年　　　　國立台灣大學公共管理學系
至 2000 年　　　主修：強調人事方面的事務行政。所修課程包括：
　　　　　　　　　　人事管理、行爲科學、組織學、心理學、勞工法。

Minors: Accounting, Finance
Secretary, Student Council, 1999 – 2000

1993 – 1996 　　Tainan Girls' High School
President, Student Council, 1995 – 1996

MISCELLANEOUS

Chief of Activity Section, China Youth Corps, 1997 – 1998
Enjoy outdoor sports, such as baseball and soccer.

REFERNCES and OTHER DETAILS　will be supplied upon request.

【 應徵職務及資格 】：

Position sought: security agent

QUALIFICATIONS: Six years in the Marine Corps, discharged
with the rank of captain. Have extensive
experience in terrorist prevention, and
was in charge of security at the R.O.C.
embassy in Korea. Qualified as an
instructor in small firearms.

** soccer〔ˈsɑkɚ〕*n.* 足球

副修：會計、財務。

1999年至2000年學生委員會祕書。

1993年　　　台南女中

至1996年　　1995年至1996年學生委員會主席。

其它方面

1997年至1998年，中國青年反共救國團活動組組長。

喜歡戶外運動，例如棒球及足球。

保證人和其它細節如有需求將會提出。

【要點說明】：在書寫所欲應徵的職務後，能再加上自己所備資格的說明，將使履歷表更具說服力。

謀求職務：安全工作人員

資　　格：　在海軍陸戰隊六年，和船長階級一同執行職務。在防禦恐怖分子上有極多的經歷，並負責駐韓國中華民國大使館的安全。小型槍砲合格教練。

The Resume

Vernon Chang

3th Fl,, 83, Lane 212, Chi-lin Rd.,
Taipei 10237   (02) 5926403

POSITION SOUGHT: COMPUTER PROGRAMMER

QUALIFICATIONS: Three years work experience operating
computer extensively, combined with
educational preparation.

EXPERIENCE:

Computer Programmer, Computer World Co., Tainan, 2006
to date.
Operate flow-charts, collect business
information for management, update methods of
operation.
Operated YBM-TX computer.

EDUCATION:

National Cheng Kung University.
Bachelor of Science, June 2006. Curriculum included:
    computer science   systems design and analysis
    FORTRAN programming   operating systems
    PASCAL programming   systems management

Kaohsiung High School, 2000 – 2003.

EXTRACARRICULAR ACTIVITIES:

National Cheng Kung University, member of computer
science club.
Kaohsiung High School, president of mathematics club.

∗∗ *flow-chart* 流程圖；流路表

英文履歷表英漢對照

張　維　能

台北市 10237 吉林路 212 巷 83 號 3 樓　　　　　　　（02）5926403

謀求職位：電腦程式設計師

資　　格：三年廣泛操作電腦的工作經驗，並有教育訓練上的準備。

經　歷：

　　2006年至今，台南世界電腦公司，電腦程式設計師
　　管理流程表，為管理收集商務資料，記下近期的操作方法。
　　操作 YBM-TX型電腦

學　歷：

　　國立成功大學
　　2006年 6 月得理學士學位。課程包括：
　　電腦科學　　　　　系統設計及分析
　　FORTRAN程式設計　作業系統
　　PASCAL程式設計　　系統管理
　　2000年至 2003 年，高雄中學

課外活動：

　　國立成功大學，電腦科學社社員
　　高雄中學，數學社社長

SKILLS:

  Examination of Data-Processing Technicians, Senior
Programmer, 2008

HOBBIES: Computer games, Chinese chess.

PERSONAL DATA:

  Born: March 10, 1985 in Kaohsiung   Health: Excellent
Marital Status: Single   Height: 172cm   Weight: 61kg

REFERENCES: Will be furnished on request.

【 經歷格式參考 】:

2006-present	Assistant loan officer at Land Bank of Taiwan. Researched customers' credit ratings and sources of collateral.
2004-2006	Teller at City Bank of Taipei. Handled customers' withdraws and deposits.
2002-2003	Typist at Evergreen Transport Corporation. Typed letters, contracts, and shipping documents.
2001-2002	Sales clerk at store 24. Stocked goods, cleaned up, and assisted the cashier.

技　　能：

　　　　2008 年，資料處理檢定考試，高級程式設計師

嗜　　好：電動玩具遊戲，象棋。

個人資料：

　　　　生日：1985 年 3 月 10 日生於高雄　　健康情形：極佳

　　　　婚姻狀況：未婚　　身高： 172 公分　　重量： 61 公斤

保　證　人：如有需求將會提出

【要點說明】：將自己的職稱和服務公司列為一行，另起一行說明職責
　　　　　　　內容，能夠達到一目瞭然之效。

2006 年至今　　　　　　台灣土地銀行借貸部主任助理。
　　　　　　　　　　　　調查客戶的信用估計及抵押品來源。

2004 年至 2006 年　　　台北市銀行出納員。
　　　　　　　　　　　　處理客戶的提款及存款。

2002 年至 2003 年　　　長榮海運公司打字員。
　　　　　　　　　　　　信件、契約、裝船文件打字。

2001 年至 2002 年　　　二十四小時商店店員。
　　　　　　　　　　　　採辦貨品，整理，並協助出納員。

The Resume

YANG LIH-JENG

10 Minchuan E. Rd.,
Taipei 10376
(02) 712-3876

Born July 11, 1974
5' 3" 109 lbs; Married
Excellent Health

OBJECTIVE: Looking for a position as a Computer Service
Technician with a medium-sized firm.

EXPERIENCE:

Description Perform both routine preventive maintenance
of Present   and diagnose and repair malfunctioning IBM
Job: computers. Used voltmeters and oscilloscopes
with job. Installed new equipment for clients.
Lay cables, hook up electrical connections
between machines, thoroughly test the new
equipments and correct the new machine. Have
up-to-date knowledge of technical information
and maintenance procedures in the industry.

Prior
Experience: An appliance repairwoman for air-conditioners
and refrigerators.

PERSONAL: Good analytical ability. Patient. Good vision
and normal perception of color. Normal hearing.
Independent. Courteous with customers.

EDUCATION: National Taipei University of Technology.
First class computer service technician,
license received in 1996.

FIRMS:

2000 - 2007 Prompt Service, Inc. Worked up to supervisory
level for Repair and Installations Department.
1998 - 2000 Datagraph Computers Sales, Co. Computer
service technician.
1996 - 1998 Computers International Co., Ltd. Computer
service technician.

ADDITIONAL PERSONAL DATA: Available to working overtime

英文履歷表英漢對照

楊　麗　珍

台北市 10376 民權東路 10 號　　　　　　　　生於 1974 年 7 月 11 日
（02）712-3876　　　　　　　　　　　　　5 呎 3 吋，109 磅；已婚
　　　　　　　　　　　　　　　　　　　　　健康情形極佳

目　　　標：　謀求一家中型公司電腦服務專門技師的職位。

經　　　驗：

當前工作敍述：　執行例行預防保養及診斷兩方面的事，並修理故障的 IBM 電腦。在工作中使用電壓表和示波器。為客戶裝設新設備。在機器間舖設電纜，裝置電的連接物，徹底測試新的設備及修正新機器。有專業技術資訊和工業程序保養的最新知識。

先 前 經 驗：　空調器及冰箱的電氣用具修理工。

個 人 資 料：　良好的分析能力，堅忍，對顏色視覺良好及感覺正常，聽力正常，獨立，對客人有禮貌。

學　　　歷：　國立台北科技大學
　　　　　　　　第一級電腦服務專門技師，1996 年收到證書。

服 務 公 司：

2000 年至 2007 年　快速服務公司，在修理裝設部門晉陞到管理階層。
1998 年至 2000 年　資料圖表電腦銷售公司。電腦服務專門技師。
1996 年至 1998 年　電腦國際有限公司。電腦服務專門技師。

另外個人資料：　可以加班

The Resume

DAVID LANG

5F No. 19 Lane 390,
Tun Hwa S. Road,
Taipei 10623

POSITION SOUGHT: ELECTRICAL ENGINEER

QUALIFICATIONS: Two years work experience performing routine engineering work, requiring application of standard techniques, procedures and criteria in carrying out a sequence of related engineering tasks. Completed graduate level studies.

EXPERIENCE: Junior Electrical Engineer at Ta Hua Engineering Works Inc. 2005-2008. Responsible for carrying out blue prints of electrical circuits of construction projects.

EDUCATION:

Tatung University
Bachelor of Science, June 2005. Curriculum included:
  Electric Power Systems   Signal Processing
  Systems and Control   Communications
  Solid-State Electronics   Electric Energy Systems
  Foundations of Systems and Control Operations
  Research
The First High School, Tainan, 1998-2001

EXTRACURRICULAR ACTIVITIES:

Tatung Institute of Technology, chairman Electrical Engineers' Society
Tainan First High School, member science Club

** criteria〔kraɪˈtɪrɪə〕 *n*. 標準；定規   *blue print* 藍圖
    curriculum〔kəˈrɪkjələm〕 *n*. 課程；功課

英文履歷表英漢對照

藍　大　衛

台北市 10623 敦化南路
390 巷 19 號 5 樓

謀求職位：電機工程師

資　　　　格：　兩年執行例行電機工作的工作經驗，需要標準技術
　　　　　　　的應用，實行一連串和電機工作相關的程序和標準。
　　　　　　　完成學士程度的課程。

經　　　　歷：　大華工程工作股份公司中級電機工程師， 2005 年
　　　　　　　到 2008 年。負責完成建築計劃電路的藍圖。

學　　　　歷

　　　大同大學
　　　2005 年 6 月獲理學士。　　課程包括：
　　　　電力系統　　　訊號處理
　　　　系統控制　　　通訊
　　　　固態電子學　　電力能源系統
　　　　基礎系統控制處理研究
　　　　1998 年至 2001 年，台南一中

課　外　活　動

　　　大同工學院，電機學會會長
　　　台南一中，科學社社員

SKILLS:

Can operate Computers. Studied Radio and TV Repair Works.

HOBBIES:

Computer Operations. Basketball. Swimming.

PERSONAL DATA:

Born: September 11, 1980 in Taichung
Health: Excellent
Marital Status: Married
Height: 5' 6"
Weight: 140 lbs.

REFERENCES: Will be furnished on request.

【結論範例】:

I believe my experiences in working with people under stressful and dangerous conditions have prepared me for working in any situation that demands interpersonal skills. I enjoy the challenge of winning people's confidence in the most trying situations. Monetary rewards are not important as long as the job keeps me interested.

技　　　　能

操作電腦。研習收音機、電視修理。

嗜　　　　好

操作電腦。籃球。游泳。

個　人　資　料

1980 年 9 月 11 日生於台中

健康情形：極佳

婚姻狀況：已婚

身高： 5 呎 6 吋

體重： 140 磅

保　　證　　人：如有需要將會提出

【要點說明】：*在履歷表最末之處，可以加上一段結論說明，往往可以收畫龍點睛之妙，標題可用 Summary, Conclusion、或者 In Conclusion.*

　　我相信我在緊張有危險的情況下，與人共事的經驗，已使我準備好在任何需要人際關係技巧的情況下工作。我喜歡在最考驗人的狀況下，贏取別人信任的挑戰。金錢的報酬並不似讓我感興趣的工作那麼重要。

The Resume

CHAU-JYE YIH

95 Tung Hwa St., Lane 34,   (02) 7023141
Taipei 10653   Born: June 12, 1978

OBJECTIVE   Position as Designs Engineer in
                   Engineering Department

QUALIFICATIONS   Work experience in a foreign engineering
                   firm coupled with educational background
                   specialized in design engineering.

EXPERIENCE

1999-Present   Worked as Product Designer for Comelco
                   Mfg. Co., Inc.
                   Responsibilities include product design
                   planning and execution.

EDUCATION

1995-1998   College of Engineering, Dept. of Industr-
                   ial Designs, Cheng Kung University,
                   Tainan. Courses taken include Simulation
                   of Dynamic Systems, Evaluation and
                   Management of Engineering Designs,
                   Tensile Structures, Systems and Control,
                   Computer-aided Design, Ergonomics,
                   Structural Analysis, Applied Mechanics.
                   Minor: Business Administration
                   Vice-President, Society for Engineers,
                   1997-1998.
1991-1995   The First High School, Tainan.
                   Secretary, Math Club, 1993-1994.

MISCELLANEOUS
                   Received Certificate for Attending Seminar
                   on Modern Products Design, University of
                   Michigan, 1998.
                   Enjoy water sports, such as scuba diving
                   and water skiing.

REFERENCES AND OTHER DATAILS will be supplied upon request.

英文履歷表英漢對照

易　超　傑

台北市 10653 通化街　　　　　　　　　（02）7023141
34 巷 95 號　　　　　　　　　　　　　生日：1978 年 6 月 12 日

| 目　　　標 | 工程部門設計工程師的職位。 |

工程部門設計工程師的職位。

資　　　格　　　外國工程公司的工作經驗，加上專攻工程設計的學
歷背景。

經　　　歷

1999 年至今　　　柯梅克製造公司，擔任產品設計者。
職務包括產品設計計劃及實行。

學　　　歷

1995 年至 1998 年　台南成功大學工學院工業設計系。修過課程包括：
動力系統外觀、工業設計評估管理、張力結構、系
統控制、電腦輔助設計、人類工程學、結構分析、
應用機械。
副修：企業管理。
1997 年至 1998 年，工程學會副會長。

1991 年至 1995 年　台南一中
1993 年至 1994 年，數學社祕書。

其 它 事 項　　　收到 1998 年密西根大學現代產品設計出席研討的
證明書。
喜歡水上活動，譬如潛水和滑水。

保證人及其它細節　如有需求將可補充。

The Resume

Jean Chiou
3F 158 Yenchi St.,
Taipei 10212
(02) 593-9847

OBJECTIVE: Job as a Magazine Writer

EXPERIENCE: Experience was acquired through summer
employment and work as an editorial assistant
of the Taipei Weekly Magazine. In college, as
the editor of the school's yearbook.

9/04-5/08 Full-time employment in Taipei Weekly
Magazine, 49 Hsin Yi Road, Sec. 2, Taipei.
Work involved: Got training in the over-all
operations of the magazine. Typed letters and
contracts, did filing and related tasks.
Also read unsolicited manuscripts and gave
recommendations for its rejection or acceptance.

5/04-8/04 Worked as a staff writer for the community
newsletter, Tien Mu Today, 80 Chung Cheng
Road Sec. 5, Tien Mu Taipei.
Wrote features for the magazine dealing with
community institutions and recreation outlets.
Also did some photography work.

ADDITIONAL
EXPERIENCE: Editor of Central University Yearbook.
Coordinated activity between editors, designers, copy editors, typesetters and other
people necessary to prepare the manuscript
for printing. Established production schedule
and set and supervised the editorial budget.

** unsolicited〔ˌʌnsəˈlɪsɪtɪd〕*adj.* 多事的；多餘的

manuscript〔ˈmænjəˌskrɪpt〕*n.* 草稿；原稿

newsletter〔ˈnjuzˌlɛtɚ, ˈnuz-〕*n.* 機關保險公司定期發行的簡訊

英文履歷表英漢對照

邱　靜
台北市 10212 延吉街 158 號 3 樓
（02）593-9847

<u>目　　　　標</u>：雜誌寫作者的工作

<u>經　　　　歷</u>：透過暑期工作，及在台北週刊雜誌擔任助理編輯得到經
驗。大學時，爲學校年鑑編輯。

04 年 9 月至　　台北週刊雜誌的全職工作。地址台北市信義路二段 49 號
08 年 5 月　　　工作包括：接受雜誌所有工作的訓練，信件及契約打字，
檔案處理及相關工作，同時也看多餘的原稿，並爲其被
拒接受給予建議。

04 年 5 月至　　擔任社區簡訊今日天母寫稿的一員，地址台北市天母中
04 年 8 月　　　正路五段 80 號。爲雜誌寫關於社區建設及消遣活動鬆弛
身心的特別報導。同時也做一些攝影的工作。

<u>其 它 經 歷</u>：中央大學年鑑編輯
協調編輯，美工，改寫編輯，排字工人及其它必須準備
原稿印刷的人員之間的事務。訂定製作進度表及調整管
理編輯預算。

EDUCATION: National Central University., major in
                   Chinese Literature, minor in English.

EXTRACURRICULAR: Member of the bowling team of school.
                   Dancing (Modern)

PERSONAL DATA: Work on overtime and on weekends
                   acceptable.

【 活動內容 】

Activities

2003-2007:   President of Toastmasters Club in Taipei.
              "Toastmasters" is dedicated to developing
              skills in public speaking. The duties of the
              president included organizing meetings,
              recruiting new members, and overseeing the
              club's finances.

2003:   Served on the advisory board to National
              Taiwan Normal University, which developed
              a unique program to give NTNU students actual
              teaching expeience in Taipei's high schools
              as part of their degree requirement.

1999-2003:   Volunteer Boy Scouts leader, brought young
              boys camping, hiking, and other scouting
              activities.

** bowling〔'bolɪŋ〕 *n.* 保齡球

學　　　歷：國立中央大學，主修中國文學，副修英文。

課 外 情 形：學校保齡球隊隊員。跳現代舞。

個 人 資 料：可以加班及在星期六工作。

【要點提示】：履歷表最主要的就是表現出自己有實力的地方。
　　　　　　　經歷較少時，也可由活動這一項來達到此一目的。

2003 年至 2007 年　　台北司儀俱樂部主席。司儀俱樂部致力於發展公衆
　　　　　　　　　　演說的技巧。主席的職責包括組織會議、招募新成
　　　　　　　　　　員、督導俱樂部的財務情形。

2003 年　　　　　　在國立台灣師範大學諮詢會裏服務，發展出一套獨
　　　　　　　　　　特的計劃，使師大學生在台北高中方面的實際教學
　　　　　　　　　　經驗成爲學位要求的一部分。

1999 年至 2003 年　　志願幼童軍領隊，帶小男孩露營、遠足、以及其它
　　　　　　　　　　的童軍活動。

The Resume

HEATHER LEHR

Personal Data: Born: November 10, 1985
Address: 20, Lane 51, Sing-Sheng S. Rd.,
      Sec. 2, Taipei 10633
Telephone: 3962337
Nationality: American

Objective: writer/proofreader

Education: University of California, Berkeley- B.A.
English 2007
Columbia University, New York, Summer 2005

Job Experience:

5/06-12/06   UNIVERSITY OF CALIFORNIA PRESS, Berkeley,
California
Editorial and Marketing Trainee.

5/06-8/06   WYATT AND DUNCAN INTERIORS, Berkeley,
California
Sales Clerk.

Summer 2004   KRAK RADIO STATION, Sacramento, California
Broadcasting and Production Trainee.

Summers 2000   QUINTESSENTIAL QUISENE, Sacramento,
California.
     2001   Caterer.

6/98-12/02   DR. LEONARD LEHR, M.D., Sacramento,
non-continuous   california
Receptionist and File Clerk.

** interior〔ɪnˈtɪrɪə〕 *n.* 室內裝潢設計師
caterer〔ˈketərə〕 *n.* 包辦酒席或餐食者

英文履歷表英漢對照

希瑟雷爾

個　人　資　料：　生日：1985 年 11 月 10 日
　　　　　　　　　住址：台北市 10633 新生南路二段 51 巷 20 號
　　　　　　　　　電話：3962337
　　　　　　　　　國籍：美國

目　　　　標：　寫作／校對

學　　　　歷：　2007 年加州柏克萊分校英語學士
　　　　　　　　2005 年夏天紐約哥倫比亞大學

工　作　經　驗：

06 年 5 月至 06 年 12 月	加州，加州大學柏克萊出版社編輯及行銷受訓員。
06 年 5 月至 06 年 8 月	加州柏克萊，偉特鄧肯室內設計店員。
2004 年夏天	加州，沙克拉孟都，克拉克電台廣播製作受訓員。
2000 年夏天 2001 年	加州，沙克拉孟都，精華料理備辦食物者。
98 年 6 月至 02 年 12 月 未繼續	加州，沙克拉孟都，李歐納德雷爾醫生處招待員暨檔案處理。

Activities:

2006   English as a Second Language tutor for
                the Bay Area Asian Youth Center. Grades 5
                through 8.

2005-2006   Founder and Editor-in-Chief of The
                Berkeley Harold, the University's humor
                magazine. Responsible for producing,
                publicizing, financing and editing the
                magazine. Managed a staff of 60 under-
                graduate and graduate students. 5 to 10
                thousand in circulation each semester.

2005-2006   Publicity director of Californians, the
                honorary service association at the
                University. Editor-in-Chief of its Big
                Game Newsletter.

2004   English Composition tutor for the YMCA.

2003-2007   Active member of the Undergraduate
                English Association.

Summer 2003   Exchange student to Greece.

Summer 2002   Exchange student to Germany.

Foreign Languages:

                Semi-Fluent in German.

                Reading knowledge of French.

                Working knowledge of Mandarin.

** publicize〔ˈpʌblɪˌsaɪz〕*v.* 宣揚；廣為宣傳
   honorary〔ˈɑnəˌrɛrɪ〕*adj.* 榮譽的

活　　　　　動：

2006 年　　　　　　海灣地區亞洲青年活動中心英語老師。
　　　　　　　　　　五級至八級。

2005 年至 2006 年　大學幽默雜誌柏克萊的哈洛得創辦者及主編。
　　　　　　　　　　負責製作、宣傳、掌理財務、編輯雜誌。管理六
　　　　　　　　　　十個大學生和研究生。每學期發行量五千至一萬
　　　　　　　　　　份。

2005 年至 2006 年　大學榮譽服務協會，加州人宣傳組長。
　　　　　　　　　　大競賽新聞簡訊主編。

2004 年　　　　　　基督教青年會英文老師。

2003 年至 2007 年　大學英語協會的活躍份子。

2003 年夏天　　　　到希臘的交換學生。

2002 年夏天　　　　到德國的交換學生。

外　　　　　語：　德語半流利。

　　　　　　　　　法語閱讀能力。

　　　　　　　　　國語應用知識。

The Resume

PETER OLIVA

3907 Vardell Road N.W.
Calgary, Alberta Canada
Telephone: (403) 288-7053

JOB OBJECTIVE   Writer

PERSONAL   Birthdate: 28-09-84 Single
                6'0"   162 lbs. Excellent Health
                Dual Citizenship: Canadian and American

EDUCATION   2002-2007   B.A. Degree in Humanities
                            Major: English
                            The University of Calgary
                            Calgary, Alberta

EDUCATIONAL
HIGHLIGHTS   English Grammar   Computer Programming
                Expository Writing   (Pascal, Assembly,
                Public Speaking   and Machine
                Speech Writing   Language)
                Creative Writing   General Psychology
                  (Fiction)   General Economics
                Canadian Liter-   Sociology of Creativity
                ature   Sociology of Work
                American Liter-   Creative Dramatics
                ature   (Teaching Children
                British Literature   Through Drama)
                                       Mandarin Chinese I

STUDENT &   Organization For Promoting English Liter-
COMMUNITY   ature
ACTIVITIES   (Department of English undergraduate club
                  hosting speakers on campus for readings
                  and lectures)
                Gauntlet University newspaper writer
                Toastmaster's Club
                  (practice in public speaking)
                Dog Training at the S.P.C.A.
                  (volunteer services)

英文履歷表英漢對照

彼得奧利瓦

加拿大　亞伯達　卡加立

瓦得爾西北路 3907 號

電話：（403）288-7053

工 作 目 標	寫作
個　　　人	生日：1984 年 9 月 28 日　　未婚 6 呎　　162 磅　　健康情形極佳 雙重國籍：加拿大和美國
學　　　歷	2002 年至 2007 年　人文學科學士 主修：英文 亞伯達卡加立大學

課程精采部分

英文文法	電腦程式設計（Pascal, As-
說明文	sembly, 和Machine lan-
公衆演說	guage）
演說寫作	普通心理學
創意寫作（小說）	普通經濟學
加拿大文學	社會創造
美國文學	社會工作
英國文學	創意戲劇（經由戲劇教導孩童）
	中文㈠

學生及社區活動

策劃提昇英國文學的活動

（英文系大學會社款請演說者到校園解說及演講。）

高利特大學新聞報寫作

司儀俱樂部（應用在公衆演說上）

S.P.C.A. 訓狗（義務服務）

EMPLOYMENT	The Galleria Arts	Part-time Sales Clerk,
03/03 - 12/07	& Crafts 1116 Memorial Drive N.W. Calgary, Alberta	Some Management, Artisan making crafts for sale
04/01 - 04/05	Hudson's Bay Company 200 8th Avenue S.W. Calgary, Alberta	Full-time Summer/Part-Time Remainder Sales Clerk, Loading Dock Worker, Computer Systems Operator in Retail Division
06/01 - 09/01	Britannia Homes Ltd. 100 Road N.W. Calgary, Alberta	Full-time Summer Construction Worker making driveways, clean-up
09/99 - 04/01	The University of Calgary Dining Centre	Part-time/Catering for large banquets and cleaning

REFERENCES   References are available on request.

INTERESTS   Enjoy writing fiction, reading, dog train-
                ing and showing dogs in competitions,
                marionette puppet making, skiing, and kick
                boxing.

IN CONCLUSION   My experience in working with people in a
                sales position and my creative background
                leave me confident in my ability to
                benefit any organization. I enjoy being
                involved and speaking in large groups and
                also find independent work rewarding and
                satisfying. I am seeking a challenging job
                opportunity.

** marionette〔,mærɪə'nɛt〕*n.* 木偶

<u>工   作</u>

03 年 3 月至 07 年 12 月	加樂利美術工藝	兼職店員
	亞伯達卡加利	部分管理，出售
	西北紀念車道 1116 號	工匠所製手工藝
01 年 4 月至 05 年 4 月	哈得森海灣公司	暑假全職／其餘時間
	亞伯達卡加利	兼職店員，碼頭裝貨
	西南第八大道 200 號	工人，零售部門電腦
		系統操作員
01 年 6 月至 01 年 9 月	布利塔尼亞家庭有限公司	暑假全職
	亞伯達卡加利	建築工作者
	西北路 100 號	建車道，清掃
99 年 9 月至 01 年 4 月	卡加利大學餐廳	兼職，為大型宴
		會配辦食物及清掃

<u>保 證 人</u>　　保證人如有需求將會用到

<u>興   趣</u>　　喜歡寫小說、閱讀、訓狗、在比賽中展示狗、製作木偶、
滑雪、打拳擊。

<u>結   論</u>　　在銷售職務上和人共事的經驗及有創造力的背景使我有
信心，我的能力會有助於任何機構。我喜歡加入大團體並
演說，同時得到獨立工作的報酬及滿足。我在找一個有
挑戰性的工作機會。

The Resume

```
AGE          : 44
DATE OF BIRTH : April 13th 1964        Martyn Green
PLACE OF BIRTH: London, England        P.O. Box 91-124
NATIONALITY   : British                Taipei, Taiwan, R.O.C.
MARITAL STATUS: Single
```

E D U C A T I O N

College & Polytechnic

Jan. '80 - Jan. '81   Croydon Technical College, South London.

Sept. '81 - May '82   Regent Street Polytechnic, London. (Institute of British Photographers' evening class course.)

University (full-time)

Sept. '89 - June '92   California State University, Fresno, California. (Majoring in Anthropology.)

Sept. '92 - Mar. '93   Columbia University, New York City. (Majoring in Film - Graduate School of Arts.)

University (part-time)

Sept. '94 - Dec. '94   University of Maryland (U.S.A.), Tehran, Iran. (Business Administration course - graded, for credit)

Feb. '96 - Mar. '96   Hong Kong University - Extramural Dept. (Psychology course)

Oct. '96 - Dec. '96   Chinese University - Extramural Dept. (Philosophy course)

Mar. '99 - May '99   Hong Kong University - Extramural Dept. (Philosophy and Psychology courses)

** polytechnic〔͵pɑlə'tɛknɪk〕*n*. 工藝學校　extramural〔͵ɛkstrə'mjʊrəl〕*adj*.校外的

英文履歷表英漢對照

年　　齡：44
生　　日：1964 年 4 月 13 日　　　　　　馬丁格林
出 生 地：英國倫敦　　　　　　　　　　中華民國台灣
國　　籍：英國　　　　　　　　　　　　台北郵政 91-124 信箱
婚姻狀況：未婚

學　　　　　歷

學 院 ‧ 工 藝 學 校

80 年 1 月至 81 年 1 月	南倫敦，克洛伊頓工業學院
81 年 9 月至 82 年 5 月	倫敦攝政街工藝學校 （英國攝影師夜間課程機構）

大 學 （ 全 時 間 的 ）

89 年 9 月至 92 年 6 月	加州福倫斯諾，加州州立大學 （主修人類學）
92 年 9 月至 93 年 3 月	紐約市哥倫比亞大學 （主修電影—藝術研究所）

大 學 （ 部 份 時 間 ）

94 年 9 月至 94 年 12 月	伊朗德黑蘭，馬里蘭大學（美國） （企管課程—給予學分）
96 年 2 月至 96 年 3 月	香港大學—為校外人士開的系 （心理課程）
96 年 10 月至 96 年 12 月	中文大學—為校外人士開的系 （哲學課程）
99 年 3 月至 99 年 5 月	香港大學—為校外人士開的系 （哲學、心理課程）

Certificates & Diplomas

1980-1981	General Certificate of Education (Ordinary Level) in Mathematics, Physics, Biology, English and General Science.
May 1982	Institute of British Photographers - Preliminary Diploma.
January 1993	Bachelor of Arts Degree in Anthropology (Magna Cum Laude), California State University, Fresno, California.

E M P L O Y M E N T

Jan. '81 - Nov. '82	Photographer's Assistant, and later, Assistant Film Editor. Associated Television, London.
Nov. '82 - Mar. '83	Assistant Newsfilm Editor Independant Television News, London.
Mar. '83 - May '86	FREELANCE Assistant Film Editor - working for: BBC Television (three times), and on such films as: "833 Squadron" (1983), "A Shot In The Dark" (1984) "Operation Crossbow" (1985), and "Dracula - Prince of Darkness" (1985) - etc.

ON FRIDAY, MAY 13th 1986, at the age of 22, I set out on a 3 1/2-year working tour around the world. Travelling mostly alone, I toured nearly 50 countries before arriving in America, to take up studies in California State University, Fresno. Jobs held on the way to the U.S. included:

VIETNAM

Aug. '87 - July '88	FREELANCE Photographer /War correspondent Associated Press and United Press International, Saigon.

** magna cum laude〔'mægnə kʌm 'lɔdɪ〕以高級優等   *set out* 出發

證　書　及　學　位

1980 年至 1981 年　　　　　數學、物理、生物、英文及普通物理
　　　　　　　　　　　　　　教育的一般證書（普通程度）

1982年5月至1993年1月　　加州福倫斯諾，加州州立大學
　　　　　　　　　　　　　　人類學學士（高級優等）

工　　　　　　　　作

81 年 1 月至 82 年 11 月　　攝影師助理，稍後，影片剪輯助理。
　　　　　　　　　　　　　　倫敦聯合電台。

82 年 11 月至 83 年 3 月　　新聞影片剪輯助理。
　　　　　　　　　　　　　　倫敦獨立電視新聞。

83 年 3 月至 86 年 5 月　　自由剪輯助理一工作：
　　　　　　　　　　　　　　BBC 電視台（三次），以及如下影片：
　　　　　　　　　　　　　　「 833 空軍中隊」（ 1983 年），
　　　　　　　　　　　　　　「胡猜瞎猜」（ 1984 年），
　　　　　　　　　　　　　　「石弓運用」（ 1985 年），
　　　　　　　　　　　　　　「黑暗王子一卓九勒」（ 1985 年）等等。

　1986 年 5 月 13 日星期五，是年 22 歲，我出發作三年半環繞世界的工作
旅行。大部分都是單獨旅行，在到達美國之前，我大約遊歷了五十個國
家，再在福倫斯諾加州州立大學繼續課程。在到美國途中繼續工作。包
括：

越　　　　　　　　　　南

87 年 8 月至 88 年 7 月　　自由攝影師／戰地記者
　　　　　　　　　　　　　　美聯社及國際合衆社，西貢

July '88 - Nov. '88　　Film Cameraman (stringer) for NBC
News, Saigon - filming and writing
own stories and recording own sound,
all over vietnam.

PART-TIME & VACATION EMPLOYMENT while a student in the
UNITED STATES.

Feb.'90 - Jul.'91　　Photographer and Media Assistant
(part-time)
Instructional Media Centre,
California State University, Fresno.

Jul.'91 - Sep.'91　　Newsfilm Cameraman and editor
(vacation)
KJEO Television, Fresno, California.

Jul.'92 -Sep.'92　　ABC News Film Cameraman (vacation -
stringer)
For ABC-affiliated stations in Los
Angeles and San Francisco.

Oct.'92 - Dec.'92　　Assistant Editor/Proof Reader
(part-time)
Ticketron "Entertainment Magazine,"
New York City.

Jun.'93 - Mar.'94　　Assistant Editor (vacation, then
permanent, staff)
NBC News, New York City.

IRAN (Recruited in New York.)

Mar.'94 - Mar.'95　　United Nations Volunteer (UNV) -
Media Specialist.
United Nations Development Programme,
Tehran, Iran.

HONG KONG (Arrived end October 1995)

Nov.'95 - Jan.'96　　FREELANCE cameraman/editor for
Farkas Studios, RTHK, and Dragon
Films.

Jan.'96 - Jul.'96　　Radio Interviewer/Reporter for RTHK
programmes:

| 88 年 7 月至 88 年 11 月 | NBC新聞影片攝影師（特約記者），西貢—把自己的故事拍寫下來，並錄下自己的聲音，遍於越南。 |

兼差及假期工作　在美國學生時代

90 年 2 月至 91 年 7 月	攝影師暨媒體助理（兼差） 福倫斯諾加州州立大學，教育媒體中心
91 年 7 月至 91 年 9 月	新聞影片攝影師及剪輯（暑假） 加州福倫斯諾KJEO電視台
92 年 7 月至 92 年 9 月	ABC新聞影片攝影師（暑假—特約記者） 洛杉磯與舊金山ABC關係電視台
92 年 10 月至 92 年 12 月	助理編輯／校對（兼差） 紐約市提克特龍「娛樂雜誌」
93 年 6 月至 94 年 3 月	助理編輯（暑假，後來長期職員） 紐約市NBC新聞

伊朗（在紐約市時加入）

| 94 年 3 月至 95 年 3 月 | 聯合國志願工作者—媒體專家
伊朗，德黑蘭，聯合國發展計劃 |

香港（1995 年 10 月底到達）

| 95 年 11 月至 96 年 1 月 | 法卡斯工作室、RTHK、龍影片公司自由攝影師／剪輯 |
| 96 年 1 月至 96 年 7 月 | RTHK無線電訪問員／記者，節目： |

	"Insight", "News Focus", "Sports Focus" and "The Kirsty Hamilton show." (Full-time freelance contributor.)
Jul.'96 - Mar.'97	Reporter, then Sub-editor and newsreader, Hong Kong Commercial Broadcasting (Commercial Radio).
May '97 - Jul.'98	Assistant Editor, "Asian Sources Electronics," Trade Media Limited.
Aug.'98 - Jan.'03	HONG KONG-BASED FREELANCE writer/ photographer, working for: Asian Business, Asia Magazine, Asiaweek, Eve Magazine, Far Eastern Economic Review, Female (Singapore), Fina (Philippines), Hong Kong Standard, Living (Singapore), Mandarin Magazine, Orientations, South China Morning Post, Style Magazine, Who Magazine (Philippines) -- etc. Also freelance radio interviewer - RTHK (HK) Also freelance film editor/cameraman /soundman -- German TV (HK), ABC News. Also Hotel Photography in Malaysia, Philippines, Sri Lanka and the Maldives.

TATWAN

Feb.'03 - Apr.'03	Studying Chinese, after moving to TAIWAN.
Jun.'03 - Sep.'03	Editor (part-time) IBS Magazine (an export, trade publication)
Oct.'03 - Feb.'04	Freelance writer/photographer
Feb.'04 - May '04	Independant Radio Producer/Presenter /Scriptwriter - "Town and Around" on ICRT, Taipei

** scriptwriter 〔'skrɪpt,raɪtə〕 *n.* 廣播稿編撰者

「洞察力」、「新焦點」、「運動焦點」、
「克絲蒂漢彌頓秀」（全職自由投稿人）

96 年 7 月至 97 年 3 月　　記者，然後是副編輯、新聞讀稿員
香港商業廣播（商業無線電播音）

97 年 5 月至 98 年 7 月　　助理編輯，「亞洲電子訊息」
貿易媒體有限公司。

98 年 8 月至 03 年 1 月　　香港—基本自由作家／攝影師，服務單位：
亞洲商業、亞洲雜誌、亞洲週刊、夏娃雜誌、
遠東經濟論談、女性（新加坡）、費娜（菲
律賓）、香港標準、生活（新加坡）、國語
雜誌、方向、南中國晨間郵報、風格雜誌、
誰雜誌（菲律賓）等等。
同時是自由無線電訪問員—RTHK（香港）
也是自由剪輯／攝影師／音效—德國電視台
（香港）
　ABC 新聞
也是馬來西亞、菲律賓、斯里蘭卡、馬爾地
夫島旅館攝影。

台　　　　　　　　　灣

03 年 2 月至 03 年 4 月　　讀中文，在搬來台灣之後。

03 年 6 月至 03 年 9 月　　編輯（兼差）IBS 雜誌（一份出口貿易刊物）

03 年 10 月至 04 年 2 月　　自由作家／攝影師

04 年 2 月至 04 年 5 月　　台北 ICRT 電台「市區及周圍」獨立無線電
播音製作／主持／廣播稿編撰者

Jun 04 - now   Freelance writer/photographer for
many of above (Aug 98 - Jan 03) Hong
Kong publications, plus: Photographer
for Asia On Line Magazine, Business
Week (U.S), International Management
(U.K.), Newsweek; also writer for
Tradewinds Magazine.

HOBBIES & INTERESTS

Computers, films, reading, travelling, listening to music,
psychology, sociology, anthropology, current affairs,
people, cross-cultural experience and walking in the
countryside.

04 年 6 月至今　　　　自由作家／攝影，上述（ 98 年 8 月至 03 年
　　　　　　　　　　1 月）香港刊物外，加上：亞洲線上雜誌、
　　　　　　　　　　商業週刊（美國）、國際管理（聯合王國）、
　　　　　　　　　　新聞週刊攝影，同時也爲貿易風雜誌寫作。

嗜　好　及　興　趣

電腦、電影、閱讀、旅行、聽音樂、心理學、社會學、人類學、時事、
人、不同的文化經驗，在鄉間散步。

【要點說明】：這是一篇英文履歷的範文實例。作者豐富的人生閱歷
　　　　　　　　及編輯、攝影的資格、能力，使此篇履歷表看來很具說
　　　　　　　　服力。一般來說，除非是經歷豐富，又都與應徵的工作
　　　　　　　　性質有密切關係時，否則履歷表的長度仍以一至二頁爲
　　　　　　　　最恰當。

The Resume

Livvy Yu
4F, 87 Sungjiang Rd.,
Taipei
(02) 592-9384

OBJECTIVE: Professor in the Foreign Language Department

EXPERIENCE: Have been working as an instructor of European studies in Chinese Culture University. Have also made some research work for the National Palace Museum in Taipei. In addition to this, have been at work on a project for the U.N. Commission on Education.

8/06-9/08   Instructor of European Studies in Chinese Culture University.
Taught junior and senior students on the methodology of historical research, French literature in the 18th century, contemporary French drama and cinema, French romanticism.

8/04-7/06   Senior researcher for the National Palace Museum in Taipei.
Conducted research on European influences on Chinese literary styles. Handled the French Department. Reported findings and gave a lecture afterwards.

3/03-4/04   Member of the UN Commission on Education for the Taiwan area. A year long work covering research on the university on Taiwan, compiled facts and statistics to be used in making a model program for other countries.

** commission〔kə′mɪʃən〕*n.* 委員會

    cinema〔′sɪnəmə〕*n.* 電影藝術；電影事業

    compile〔kəm′paɪl〕*v.* 搜集並編輯

英文履歷表英漢對照

余 麗 薇
台北市松江路 87 號 4 樓
（02）592-9384

目　　　標：　　外文系教授

學　　　歷：　　曾任中國文化大學歐洲研究講師。同時在台北
　　　　　　　國立故宮博物院做過一些研究工作。除此之外，
　　　　　　　曾進行聯合國教育委員會的計劃。

06 年 8 月至 08 年 9 月　　中國文化大學歐洲研究講師。教導大三大四學
　　　　　　　生歷史研究方法論、十八世紀法國文學、當代
　　　　　　　法國戲劇及電影藝術、法國浪漫主義。

04 年 8 月至 06 年 7 月　　台北國立故宮博物院高級研究員。
　　　　　　　在歐洲對中國文學風格影響方面作研究。處理
　　　　　　　法國部門。之後報告發現及作演講。

03 年 3 月至 04 年 4 月　　聯合國教育委員會台灣地區會員。為期一年的
　　　　　　　工作包括研究台灣的大學，搜集並編輯實際狀
　　　　　　　況和統計數字，用來作為其它國家的典範計畫。

Education: Graduate Course at Tamkang University.
2001-2004   Received the degree of Master of French
                  Literature
1997-2001   French major at Fu Jen Catholic University,
                  minor in Spanish.

EXTRACURRICULAR: Member of the Green Earth Movement and
                  the Society for the Advancement of Art
                  and Literature in Taiwan.

PERSONAL DATA: Prefer to work at night.

【 工作經歷 】：

EXPERIENCE: Extensive experience in all aspects of
                  show business. Was a actress in numerous
                  productions at the National Theater. Was a
                  script writer for the soap opera "All My
                  Children" on TV. And have worked as a model
                  for ABC modeling Agency.

12/07-present: On the acting staff of the National
                  Theater. Played a leading role in the
                  production of "A Journey to the West,"
                  which was highly praised by critics.

9/04-12/07:   Was on the writing staff for Taiwan
                  Television Enterprise(TTV). Co-wrote the
                  script of "All My Children," which won the
                  Golden Bell Award. Also co-wrote the soap
                  operas "The Days of Our Lives" and "General
                  Hospital."

1/03-9/04:   Worked for ABC modelling Agency, 10
                  Chunghsiao East Road, Section 2, Taipei.
                  Appeared on television in commercials
                  promoting hair spray.

學　　　歷：

| 2001 年至 2004 年 | 淡江大學研究課程。獲法國文學碩士學位。 |
| 1997 年至 2001 年 | 輔仁大學主修法文，副修西班牙文。 |

課　　　外：　　　綠化土地運動及台灣文學藝術促進學會會員。

個 人 資 料：　　　晚上工作尤佳。

【要點提示】：Chronological Resume 的重點在於工作的經歷是依時間順序來排列的，適合於有多年工作經驗的人用。

經　　　　　歷：　　在各層面的表演事業上有廣泛的經驗。國立劇場極多戲碼的女演員。電視連續劇「我的孩子們」腳本作者。ABC模特兒代理公司模特兒。

07 年 12 月至今：　　國立劇場演員陣容。「西遊記」中扮演極重要的角色，受到評論很高的讚譽。

04 年 9 月至 07 年 12 月：　為台灣電視公司寫作。合作寫「我的孩子們」的腳本，獲得金鐘獎，同時合作寫出「我們的日子」及「綜合醫院」連續劇。

03 年 1 月至 04 年 9 月：　ＡＢＣ模特兒公司工作，地址台北市忠孝東路二段十號。
於電視廣告中促銷頭髮噴霧劑。

The Resume

RESUME of

MEI-YU CHAO

195 Minsheng E. Road,   (02) 762-3155
Taipei 10205   Born: Oct. 1, 1982

OBJECTIVE

A position as English Instructor, preferably handling
students from the intermediate to the advance levels.

QUALIFICATIONS

Four years working experience in teaching English in
Japan coupled with educational background specialized in
English Instruction.

EXPERIENCE

2005-Present   English Instructor at Nagoya University,
                 English Department.
                 Taught Creative Writing, English Literature

2004-2005   Teacher's aide in Mckinley School, Oahu,
                 Honolulu.

EDUCATION

2001-2005   National Taiwan University, Department of
                 Foreign Languages and Literatures. Courses
                 taken: English Literature. Teaching English
                 as a Second Language. Methodology of
                 Teaching. International Education. English
                 Education. Reading. English Club member.

1997-2001   The First High School, Tainan
                 Class President, 1999-2000

REFERENCES AND OTHER DETAILS TO BE SUPPLIED UPON REQUEST

** methodology〔͵mɛθəd'ɑlədʒɪ〕*n*. 方法論；課程論

英文履歷表英漢對照

履　歷　表

趙　美　玉

台北市 10205　　　　　　　　　　　（02）762-3155
民生東路 195 號　　　　　　　　　生日：1982 年 10 月 1 日

目　　　標

英文老師的職位，最好能帶領中級至高級程度的學生。

資　　　格

四年在日本教英文的經驗，加上專攻英語教學的學歷背景。

經　　　歷

2005 年至今　　　　名古屋大學英文系英文老師
　　　　　　　　　　教創意寫作，英國文學
2004 年 2005 年　　檀香山歐胡島麥克金利高中助教。

學　　　歷

2001 年至 2005 年　國立台灣大學，外國語文學系。
　　　　　　　　　　修過課程：英國文學、英語教學法、教學方法論、
　　　　　　　　　　國際教育、英語教育、閱讀。英語俱樂部會員。
1997 年至 2001 年　台南一中
　　　　　　　　　　班長，1999 年至 2000 年

保證人和其它細節如有要求將會補充

The Resume

Qualifications of Su-ling Teng

5F-2 No. 19,
Hsin Sheng S. Road, Sec. 2,   (02) 359-6273
Taipei 10299

Position applied for: Research Assistant

EXPERIENCE

2007-Present   Marketing Research specialist of Market
                Facts, Taipei, Inc.
                Responsibilities include:
                1) Design research projects.
                2) Analyze and interpret results.
                3) Make recommendations based on results
                   of research.
2005-2007   Selling Areas-Marketing, Inc., Taipei.
                Public relations officer.
                Responsibilities include:
                1) Promotion of certain personalities
                   through arranging media contacts.
                2) Travel arrangements for VIPS.
2003-2005   Assistant account trainee for Klein-Kramer
                Company, Taipei.
                Responsibilities include:
                1) Maintain Files.
                2) Answer Phones.
                3) Research and assemble information for
                   speeches and pamphlets.
                4) Scan and clip newspaper and magazine
                   articles.
                5) Type.
                6) Prepare media list.

** media〔′mɪdɪə〕*n.* 大眾傳播工具   *VIP* 重要人物 (= *very important person*)
   pamphlet〔′pæmflɪt〕*n.* 小冊子
   scan〔skæn〕*v.* 匆匆地略看   clip〔klɪp〕*v.* 剪

英文履歷表英漢對照

鄧淑玲所備資格

台北市 10299 新生南路
二段 19 號 5 樓之 2

（02）359-6273

應徵職位：研究助理

經　　　　　歷

2007 年至今　　　市場實情台北公司，市場研究專家
　　　　　　　　　職務包括：
　　　　　　　　　1）設計研究計劃。
　　　　　　　　　2）分析並解釋結果。
　　　　　　　　　3）根據研究結果作建議。

2005 年至 2007 年　台北銷售領域——市場公司，公共關係職員。
　　　　　　　　　職務包括：
　　　　　　　　　1）透過安排媒體接觸，宣傳某些人物。
　　　　　　　　　2）為重要人物安排旅行。

2003 年至 2005 年　台北克連克倫摩公司助理會計見習生。
　　　　　　　　　職務包括：
　　　　　　　　　1）持續檔案。
　　　　　　　　　2）接電話。
　　　　　　　　　3）研究安排演講和小冊子的資料。
　　　　　　　　　4）約略閱覽報章雜誌的專論並剪下來。
　　　　　　　　　5）打字。
　　　　　　　　　6）準備媒體清表。

EDUCATION

2001-2003   Department of Communications Management,
                  Shih-Hsin University.
                  Courses taken: History of mass communic-
                  ations, China's communication history,
                  Media research, Consumer information
                  seeking and processing behaviors, Public
                  opinion, Conceptual analysis, New methods
                  of communication research, Content
                  analysis, Advertising, New media
                  technology.
1997-2001   Ping-Tung Girls' High School.

SKILLS   Typing 50 wpm, Basic knowledge of
                  computers, Drive a Car.

PERSONAL DATA   Born July 8, 1980   5'5", 130 lbs.
                  Married   Excellent Health

REFERENCES AND FURTHER DENTAILS TO BE FURNISHED UPON
REQUEST

【工作經歷例文】：

EXPERIENCE: Have teaching experience at Giant Cram
                  School and also taught privately. Served
                  as a teaching assistant in college.

10/04-present: Full time teacher at Giant Cram School,
                  31 Hoping East Road, Section 2. Was voted
                  the best teacher by students in 2006. Over
                  80 percent of my students have gained
                  acceptance to college.

10/04-9/07:   Gave private instruction to students at
                  their homes. The college acceptance rate
                  of my private students has been 100 percent.

ADDITANAL   In college was a teaching-assistant for
EXPERIENCE: the Cram School. Helped unsatisfactory
                  students who were in danger of flunking.

學　　　　　　歷

2001 年至 2003 年　　世新大學傳播管理學系

　　　　　　　　　　修過課程：大衆傳播史，中國傳播史，媒體研究，
　　　　　　　　　　消費者資訊搜尋及程序行爲，輿論學，觀念分析，
　　　　　　　　　　傳播研究新法，內容分析，廣告學，新媒體方法。

1997 年至 2001 年　　屏東女中

技　　　　　　能　　每分鐘打字 50 字，電腦基本知識，開車。

個　人　資　料　　1980 年 7 月 8 日生　　　5 呎 5 吋　　　130 磅
　　　　　　　　　已婚　　　　　　　　　　健康情形極佳

保證人及另外的細節如有需要將補充

【工作經歷例文】：

經　　　　　　驗：　　有任教於巨人補習班的經驗，同時私底下授課。
　　　　　　　　　　在大學時擔任助教。

04 年 10 月至今　：　　巨人補習班全職老師，地址和平東路二段三十
　　　　　　　　　　一號。2006 年時被學生選爲優良老師。百分
　　　　　　　　　　之八十以上的學生爲學校錄取。

04年10月至07年9月：　　在學生家中給予個人的指導。私授的學生錄取
　　　　　　　　　　率爲百分之百。

其　它　經　驗：　　在大學時是補習班的助教。幫助有被當掉危險
　　　　　　　　　　的不合格學生。

The Resume

Wen-in Fu
Age 25(January 5, 1984)
Single, Excellent health

3, Hoping E. Road, Sec. 3
Taipei 10112
(02) 341-7133

OBJECTIVE

Position in the Executive Management team as an Executive Interpreter

QUALIFICATIONS

Good university education combined with practical experience in translating business documents and have done extensive travelling.

EMPLOYMENT

2005-Present   Sino Trading Co., Ltd. Kaohsiung. Accompanied Company president on trips abroad as his translator. Supervised the export division of company in handling customers and foreign documents. Helped negotiate business transactions of the company with foreign clients.

2004-2005   McNeil Publishing House. Liaison Officer of said company in Taiwan.

EDUCATION

2000-2004   Department of English, Fu Jen University. Major: English----Second Language Education, Bilingual Education, English Education, Technical Communication, English for Special Purposes, English Structure, American Culture and Literature.

1996-2000   Fu-Shing High School, Taipei.

** liaison 〔,lie′zɔ̃〕 *n.* 聯絡

英文履歷表英漢對照

履 歷 表

傅文英　　　　　　　　　　　　　　台北市 10112
25 歲（1984 年 1 月 5 日）　　　　　和平東路三段 3 號
未婚，健康情形極佳　　　　　　　　（02）341-7133

目 標
執行管理小組執行翻譯的職務

資 格
好的大學教育，加上翻譯商業文件的實務經驗，並曾四處旅行。

工 作

2005 年至今　　　　　高雄西諾貿易有限公司
　　　　　　　　　　　跟隨公司董事長旅行國外，作為翻譯
　　　　　　　　　　　管理公司出口部門，處理顧客及外國的文件
　　　　　　　　　　　協助公司與外國客戶交涉商務處理
2004 年至 2005 年　　麥克尼爾出版社。前述公司台灣聯絡員

學 歷

2000 年至 2004 年　　輔仁大學英文系
　　　　　　　　　　　主修：英文……第二語言教育，雙語教育，英
　　　　　　　　　　　　　　　文教育，專業溝通，特殊目的
　　　　　　　　　　　　　　　用英語，英語結構，美國文化
　　　　　　　　　　　　　　　及文學。
1996 年至 2000 年　　台北復興高中

EXTRACURRICULAR ACTIVITIES

Representative to Student Council, Fu Jen University, 2003

SKILLS   Typing, 40wpm. Water color Painting.

REFERENCES Will be supplied on request.

【 工作經歷格式參考 】:

2003- present	Far East Trading Company 117 Nanking East Road, Sec. 1 Taipei	Regional Sales Manager: responsible for sales to the European market.
2001-2003	Lee's Export Unlimited 81 Chunghsiao East Road, Sec 2 Taipei	Secretary: typed, an- swered the telephone, arranged appointments and handled routine paper-work.
2000-2001	The China Garden Restaurant 9 Minchuan Road, Sec 1 Taipei	Waitress: waited on customers.
1999-2000	Welcome Supermarket 20 Hsinyi Road, Sec 3 Taipei	Cashier

課 外 活 動

輔仁大學學生會代表，2003 年

技 能　　　　　打字每分鐘 40 字，水彩畫。

保 證 人　　　　如有需求將可補充。

【要點說明】：對於有豐富工作經驗的人而言，履歷表的重心就是列出
　　　　　　以往的工作記錄。三段式的格式非常的清楚明白。

2003 年至今	遠東貿易公司 台北市南京東路 一段 117 號	區域性行銷經理： 負責行銷到歐洲市場
2001 年至 2003 年	李氏出口無限公司 台北市忠孝東路 二段 81 號	祕書：打字、接聽電話、安排約會、處理例行文件。
2000 年至 2001 年	中國園餐廳 台北市民權東路一段 9 號	女服務生：服務顧客
1999 年至 2000 年	歡迎光臨超級市場 台北市信義路三段 20 號	出納員

The Resume

JIEH-CHYI LAI

6F 89 Hsin Sheng S. Rd., Sec. 3   Born January 9, 1981
Taipei 10715   5' 8" 140 lbs; Married
(02) 341-7754   Excellent health

OBJECTIVE: To serve as a general manager in a man-
                  ufacturing concern. Scope of work to
                  include a lot of field work and meeting
                  clients.

QUALIFICATIONS: Has received M.B.A. from Kogod College of
                  Business Administration, American Univer-
                  sity. Did practicum in an American company.
                  In Taiwan, worked for Solomon Brothers,
                  Taipei.

EXPERIENCE: Administrative assistant to the General
                  manager of Solomon Brothers, Taipei.
2008-present   Handled the itinerary schedule of the
                  general manager of Solomon Brothers. Met
                  clients as a representative of the com-
                  pany. Help negotiate a US$400,000 deal
                  for the company.
2006-2008   Gracewald Toys Ltd. Learned about American
                  accounting systems and office procedures.
                  Earned high praise for my diligence and
                  fast results.

EDUCATION:

2004-2006   Master of Business Administration at
                  Kogod College of Business Administration,
                  American University, 4400 Massachusetts
                  Avenue, NW Washington, D.C. 20016
2000-2004   Economics major at Chung Yuan Christian
                  University, Chung Li.

SKILLS: Computer Programmer Fortran.

REFERENCES: To be furnished upon request.

** scope〔skop〕*n.* 活動或觀察的範圍   itinerary〔aɪˈtɪnə,rɛrɪ,ɪ-〕*n.* 旅行計畫

英文履歷表英漢對照

賴 介 琦

台北市 10715
新生南路三段 89 號 6 樓
（02）341-7754

生於 1981 年 1 月 9 日
5 呎 8 吋，140 磅；已婚
健康情形極佳

目　　　標：	擔任製造股份公司的總經理。工作的活動範圍包括很多領域的業務及會見客戶。
資　　　格：	獲美國大學科嘉企業管理學院企業管理碩士。在一家美國公司實習。在台灣，爲台北所羅門兄弟公司服務。
經　　　歷：	台北所羅門兄弟公司總經理之行政助理。
2008 年至今	處理所羅門兄弟公司總經理旅行計畫時間表。作爲公司代表接見客戶。協助公司交涉了四十萬美元的交易。
2006 年至 2008 年	葛雷絲瓦得玩具有限公司。學到關於美國會計系統及辦公室程序。我的勤勉及成效快速贏得高度讚賞。
學　　　歷：	
2004 年至 2006 年	華盛頓西北哥倫比亞特區 20016 麻塞諸賽大道 4400 號 美國大學科嘉企業管理學院企管碩士
2000 年至 2004 年	中壢中原大學主修經濟
技　　　能：	FORTRAN 電腦程式。
保　　　證　　人：	如有需求將會補充。

How to
Write a
Successful
Resume

第五篇

英文履歷表的
最佳拍檔
附　　函

1. 穿針引線的地位

2. 附函的檢查清單

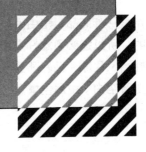

How to Write a Successful Resume

1. 穿針引線的地位

　英文履歷表一定要附上附函（***Cover Letter***），也就是自薦函，是一種把自己銷售出去的銷售函件。所以一定要能引起雇主的注意，繼而訂出與你面談的時間。寫法依照商業書信的原則，簡潔、明瞭、具體，並注意收信人姓名、地址、及信封上的寫法。

附函的目的

　寄英文履歷表時，如果沒有附上附函，是一種**失禮**的表現，而且沒有辦法得到效果。而且附函必須配合特定的雇主及依不同的應徵工作有不同的內容，給雇主有清晰而良好的印象，才能爭取到面試的機會。

　附函中可以談談想應徵的工作和自己的資格，不拘泥於形式，但是要儘量簡單，可以僅僅敘述要求面試機會的要點。如果履歷表中因經歷較少而顯得空洞，就把較難寫在履歷表中的願望、能力、資質等，一併寫入附函中。

　把自己當作是一件商品，藉由附函這種銷售函件推銷出去，就算達到了附函的目的。所以還必須寫好安排了面試事宜的**回郵信封**（也就是要寫好自己的姓名、住址、貼好郵票）及**回函明信片**（寫下必要事項，並在面試時間處留空白，由雇主填寫）一起寄去，如此可以節省對方的時間，並留下一個好印象。

附函的形式

　　附函和英文履歷表一樣，它的格式往往可以決定第一印象，因此版面格式不可不留意。

　　紙張的大小和英文履歷表一樣採用 A4 紙，它的形式可依商業書信的形式，分爲下列四種：

① 齊頭式　*Block Form*

　　每一行都從左邊開始，對打字員而言，是最不費力的形式，但和其它形式比較起來，有偏左的感覺。

② 變體齊頭式　*Modified Block Form*

　　把 Block Form的日期、結尾的客套話及簽名的位置放在右邊，標題挪到中間的位置。

③ 折衷式　*Semi-block Form*

　　和上述的Modified Block Form是美國目前很普遍的兩種格式，唯一和Modified Block Form不同之處，是每一行的開始，必須先縮進數格。

④ 鋸齒式　*Indented Form*

　　這是英國的標準格式，整個形式很好看，但是內縮的次數太多，很花時間。

　　以下是商業書信的四種形式。

① Block Form

② Modified Block Form

③ Semi-block Form

④ Indented Form

附函的版面設計及寫法

Semi-block Form :

28-5, San-do 3rd Rd,
Kaohsiung, 80216

May 10, 2008

Mr. John S. Mill
Personnel Manager
Taping Co., Ltd,
20, Fu-hsing S. Rd.,
Taipei 10275

Dear Mr. Mill:

Sincerely yours,

Victor Lai

前面是 Semi-block form 的版面，根據它，稍微簡單說明信函各要素的寫法。

① 地址

要把自己的住址寫在最上面的右邊，住址最好能加上郵遞區號。

② 日期

日期寫在地址下面二到三行處靠右邊的地方。至於日期的寫法則有下面幾種：

- 美式── **May 8, 2008**　　　 ·英美共通── **8 May, 2008**
- 英式── **8th May, 2008**；**May 8th, 2008**

③ 收信人姓名住址

收信人的姓名和住址寫在日期下面四到五行處，如果是簡短的文章，就要更下面，而且是從離左邊兩公分的地方開始寫。可以寫出對方的姓名和頭銜，如果不知道姓名時，則必須要寫出頭銜，但以寫出姓名為佳。

④ 信的開端稱呼

稱呼寫在姓名地址下方二到三行處。如果知道對方姓名，可以寫成 *Dear Mr. Huang*:，但不要稱呼對方的名字（*first name*）。不知道對方姓名，可書寫如下：

- 美式　**Dear Sir:**　　　 ·英式　**Dear Sir,**

如果是公司的信件，就寫成：

- 美式　**Gentlemen:**　　　 ·英式　**Dear Sirs,**

⑤ 本文

本文從信的開端稱呼下面一行開始寫起，行間距離也是一行。

⑥ 書信結尾的客套話

結尾的客套話寫在本文下一行的地方，寫法如下：

- 美式　**Sincerely yours**, 或是 **Yours very truly,**

・英式　**Yours Faithfully,**

起首則從離日期左邊再左一點的位置開始。

⑦ **姓名**

簽名儘量寫在結尾客套話下面三行處，而且是用打字的，起首也和結尾客套話齊平。

收信人姓名・住址

如果不是親友介紹或看報上刊登的廣告，而是自己單方面去求職的話，就要寫出那公司內最恰當的人名。

小公司的話是總經理，規模較大的公司寫法如下：

① 應徵的是中級職務，就寫相關部門的主管，譬如是經理部門的工作，可以寫

　　* Mr. Ivan Hong　　　　　　　　　　會計部經理

　　Manager, Accounting Department　　洪伊文先生

② 應徵基層人員的工作時，就寫人事主管。

　　* Mr. Chung-hwa Chan, Personnel Manager

　　人事經理，詹中華先生

③ 應徵一般工作時，只要寫

　　* Personnel Department ……………………………… 人事部門

④ 如果想應徵的工作有特定的範圍，最好寫該部門的主管。如果具備特別的檢定資格，就寫有關連的部門主管。

本　文

銷售信件的寫法，有AIDA的原則：

A　Attention（注意）　　I　Interest（興趣）

D　Desire（願望）　　　A　Action（行動）

　　這也同樣適用於附函，因為附函的目的在於爭取面試的機會。所以首先要引起雇主的注意，對你關心，並且想和你面談，最後安排了面談的機會。

① 引起注意——內文的起首

　　內文的起首，因別人介紹、看應徵廣告、或自己來應徵等情況而有不同。下面分別舉例說明：

A. 別人介紹時，也要把情形說清楚。

　　（一）Mr. James Brown of your company has told me that you need additional staff member for your Accounting Department.

　　　　貴公司的詹姆斯‧布朗先生告訴我，貴公司需要增加會計部成員。

＊　　　　＊　　　　＊

　　（二）Professor Chung-I Lee of Taiwan University suggested that I apply for a position with your company as an accountant.

　　　　台灣大學的李忠義教授建議我應徵貴公司的會計職位。

B. 看應徵廣告，同樣地要把情形寫清楚。

　　（一）With reference to your advertisement in today's China Times for a secretary, I wish to apply for the position.

　　　　參考今天中國時報上貴公司廣告徵求祕書，我想要應徵這個職位。

＊　　　　＊　　　　＊

　　（二）Post of Secretary（China Times, March 23, 2008）

　　　　I shall be glad if you consider me for the position.

　　祕書職位（2008 年 3 月 23 日，中國時報）

　　我會很高興，如果貴公司在這職位上考慮用我。

＊ 　　　　 ＊ 　　　　 ＊

（三）I wish to apply for the position of secretary which you advertised in China Times, March 30, 2008.

　　我想要應徵貴公司 2008 年 3 月 30 日在中國時報所刊登的祕書一職。

　　以上所舉的例子是普遍的起首，下面則摘要寫出學歷及經歷方面的資格。

　　Courses in secretarial science and two years experience in a foreign affiliated firm qualify me to apply for the position of the secretary that you advertised in the China Times, March 31, 2008.

　　祕書知識方面的課程及在外商公司兩年的工作經驗，使我具備了貴公司在 2008 年 3 月 31 日中國時報所刊登祕書一職的應徵資格。

C. 不經他人介紹或應徵廣告，而是自己去應徵的，這種情形就要強調求職的意志。

（一）I am applying for a position with your company as an accountant as I feel my experience in accounting with a major trading firm will be useful to your organization.

　　我來應徵貴公司的會計職位。因為我覺得我在大型貿易公司的經驗會對貴公司有所助益。

＊ 　　　　 ＊ 　　　　 ＊

（二）Since your company is one of the leading foreign-capital banks in Taiwan, I would like to put my financial training and experience to work for you.

由於貴公司是台灣主要的外資銀行之一，我想以我財務方面的
訓練和經驗，來爲貴公司效勞。

＊　　　　　＊　　　　　＊

(三) As you can see by the enclosed resume, I will be graduating next June from Chengchi University and I am
interested in finding a secretarial job in an American
affiliated bank.

您可以在所附的履歷表中看到，我將在明年六月由政治大學畢
業，而且我對於在美商銀行覓得祕書一職非常感興趣。

＊　　　　　＊　　　　　＊

(四) Congratulations on the opening of Fashion Apparel Import Department. Because of my background and interest in the import of high fashion wear, I am applying
for a managerial position in the new department.

恭禧流行服飾進口部門開張。因爲對進口高級流行服飾具有經
歷及興趣，所以我來應徵新部門的經理職位。

② 引起關心

接下來要挑出自己最大的銷售要點（*sales point*），讓雇主知道
你對他有什麼幫助，你的資格又對職務有什麼關係。沒有經歷或經歷
少時，學歷就是最大的銷售要點。

《學歷》

My education has given me a broad background in the
field of foreign trade. Courses in business communication provided me with an understanding of effective
business communication in cross-cultural settings and,
in my foreign trade courses, primary emphasis was
placed on realistic import and export transactions.

學校教育給了我外貿方面廣泛的知識背景。商務溝通的課程使我了解另一種文化環境中有效的商務溝通，而且我的外貿課程主要在強調實際的進出口處理。

這一部分和下面的部分，是附函的重心所在，非常重要，它也是最能夠看出求職者個性的憑據，寫法則因人而異。

③ 表示你的希望

除了上述的銷售要點和應徵工作有關連外，還有工作的經歷、工讀、對於對方公司及相關業務的關心。如果對應徵的工作沒有太多的經驗，就強調願意接受工作的挑戰，能夠適應新環境，學習積極，並具有與人相處的協調性等等。

≪工作經驗≫

During my summer-job with Tonho Trading Co., I gained a great deal of first-hand knowledge about foreign trade, and through my work experience I learned how to work with people of different interests and backgrounds.

在東和貿易公司暑期工讀時，我獲得相當多關於外貿方面的第一手知識，並且透過工作經驗，我學習到如何和不同興趣背景的人一塊兒工作。

在接近結尾的部分，提到英文履歷表時，

* A resume is enclosed for your examination.
附上一份履歷表供您查閱。

不可以像此例一樣，寫得那麼簡單，而要把履歷表內容的重點，加以說明。

《强調履歷表》

My resume shows success in coordinating a busy schedule of collegiate studies, part-time jobs, and extracurricular activities. The presidency of the Student
Council provides evidence of the trait which you re-
quire: the capacity of cooperation and leadership.

我的履歷表說明了我能成功地調配大學課業，兼差的工作，及
課外活動的繁忙時間。學生會會長的任職能證明貴公司要求的
特性：合作及領導的能力。

④ 希望對方採取行動——結尾

最後，要提到你希望能夠有面試的機會。電話號碼雖然已寫在履
歷表了，但在附函裏最好能夠再提一下，這會帶來很好的效果。

《結尾1》

Although this letter and resume give you some idea of
my qualifications, I am eager to talk with you. Please
call me at 703 — 5833 after 6 p.m. on any weekday. I
am looking forward to hearing from you.

雖然這封信函及履歷表使您對我的資格有些了解，但我非常希
望與您談談。週一至週六下午六時以後請電 7035833。期盼接
到您的消息。

《結尾2》

Will you allow me a chance to discuss the qualifications
required for the job? For an interview at your convenience, please call 7014887 between 7 and 9 p.m. Monday
through Friday or write to my home address.

對於這份工作所要求的資格，您能不能給我一個機會與您討論?
依您的方便見面，星期一至星期五請於下午七時至九時電 701-
4887，或寫信至我家。

　　如果是自己去應徵工作，沒有透過報上廣告或經由別人介紹的附函，
結尾可以書寫如下：

≪結尾 3 ≫

Please consider me for the position when a vacancy in
your company becomes available. I will be glad if we
could set an appointment, and you can get to know me
better. Therefore, my resume is enclosed with this
letter. Thank you for your attention, and I look forward to hearing from you soon.

當貴公司有職缺時，請把我列入考慮。我會很高興如果我們能
訂個會面的時間，那麼您可以對我這個人知道得更清楚。隨信
附寄我的履歷表。謝謝您的注意，並盼望很快有您的回音。

≪結尾 4 ≫

If you have any openings please let me know. I would
be happy with any position that you are offering. I've
enclosed my resume, but I request the opportunity for
an interview so we can meet personally. You may reach
me at 713—5429 after 7 p.m. Look forward to hearing
from you as soon as possible.

如果貴公司有任何的職缺請通知我，我會很樂意去作貴公司所
提供的任何職位。附寄上我的履歷表，但我要求一個面試的機
會，好讓我們能當面會晤。您可以在七點之後打 713－5429 給
我。期待您儘速的回訊。

How to Write a Successful Resume

2. 附函的檢查清單

　　從你所寄出的附函就可以知道你對商業書信寫法了解到什麼程度。按照這幾點全部檢查一遍，這是非常重要的。

① 體裁

☆ 使用質地好的白紙嗎？

☆ 形式正確嗎？

☆ 版面有吸引力嗎？

☆ 有沒有拼錯字，文法對不對，紙張乾淨嗎？

② 內容

☆ 有沒有寫雇主的姓名？

☆ 有沒有回函信封、上面的姓名、地址有沒有寫清楚？

☆ 是否能引起閱讀者的注意？

☆ 使用的字句能給人最好的印象嗎？

☆ 是否具體地寫出你的職務？

☆ 有沒有寫出應徵該工作的理由？

☆ 有沒有寫出讓人相信你有資格的理由？

☆ 有沒有寫最大的銷售要點？

☆ 有沒有說明英文履歷表的要點？

☆ 有沒有強調和工作有關的資格？

☆ 有沒有寫出你的經歷、教育、性格對工作能有什麼幫助？

☆ 有沒有提到附在信內的英文履歷表？

☆ 有沒有要求面試？

☆ 有沒有寫電話號碼及方便的時間？

③ **態度**

☆ 是不是站在雇主的立場上來寫的？

☆ 有沒有表現出求職的關心與熱誠？

☆ 有沒有儘量避免使用第一人稱？

☆ 能不能給與人家安全的感覺？

HOUR PROCESSIN

How to
Write a
Successful
Resume

第六篇

附函範例

The Cover Letter

2nd Fl., 24,
Lane 95, Yung-kang st.,
Taipei 10625

May 5, 2008

Ms. Roy Burke
Personnel Department
Taiwan Prentice Co., Ltd.
3rd Fl., 7, Alley 13,
Lane 150, Jen-ai Rd., Sec 2,
Taipei 10257

Dear Ms. Burke:

With my thorough secretarial and accounting training background, I wish to apply for an entry-level secretarial position.

My training at Ming Chuan University, coupled with summer and part-time work experience have helped me develop these skills and I would like to have a chance to explain how I can put them to work for your organization.

Ever since I studied management in the University, I have done well both in secretarial studies and accounting, and I am very interested in both fields.

The position which offers an opportunity to utilize my training in these two fields will be ideal for me; but enthusiasm, and sincere desire to become an administrative secretary are the driving force of my career plans.

The enclosed resume describes my education and work experience, but I would like to discuss the possibility with you soon. May I have an interview? I look forward to your call at 3965248 or your letter to the above address.

Sincerely yours,

Fanny Chan

附函英漢對照

台北市 10625 永康街 95 巷
24 號 2 樓

2008 年 5 月 5 日

台北市 10257 仁愛路二段
150 巷 13 弄 7 號 3 樓
台灣普倫提斯有限公司人事室
洛伊柏克先生收

親愛的柏克先生：

　　由於充份的祕書及會計訓練背景，我希望能應徵一個初級祕書的職位。

　　我在銘傳大學接受的訓練，及暑假打工兼差的工作經驗幫助我培養了這些有關技能，我很希望有機會向您說明我將如何在貴機構運用這些技能。

　　打從我在大學學管理起，我的祕書課程及會計成績就不錯，而且我對這兩科相當感興趣。

　　這個職位提供我利用這兩方面訓練的機會，對我來說非常理想；但熱切及誠心地想成為一個行政祕書才是我事業計畫的推動力。

　　附帶的簡歷略述了我的教育背景及工作經驗，但我希望能很快地與您討論工作的可能性。我可否有個面談機會？期待您電 3965248 或來信至上述地址。

　　　　　　　　　　　　　　　　　　　詹芬妮　敬上

The Cover Letter

161, Lane 191
King-shan S. Rd., Sec. 2
Taipei 10722

June 1, 2008

Mr. Ivan Fei
Personnel Manager
Yung-An Ltd.
11th Fl., 59
Hsinyi Rd., Sec.3
Taipei 10422

Dear Mr. Fei:

I believe my education, training and personal qualities
give me the background you desire for the position of
executive assistant you advertised in the China Times
News of May 27.

My seven years of continuous secretarial experience,
out of which five years have been with foreign-affiliated
companies, have taught me how to do all phases of office
work. Because of the rather small staff of the companies
where I worked, I have carried out many different
responsibilities. I can type, handle paperwork and
correspondence, operate a switchboard and act as a
receptionist.

I believe I have the personal qualities that would fit
me in harmoniously with your firm. I like people and
through experience I have learned how to work with them.
I like to be challenged with a job that provides variety,
new tasks and responsibilities.

The enclosed resume will give you details about my
background. May I come to see you at your convenience to
disccuss the possibility? Please call me at 281-1882.

Sincerely yours,

Hsiao-ch'i Chou

** *carry out* 完成；實行

附函英漢對照

台北市 10722 金山南路
二段 191 巷 161 號
2008 年 6 月 1 日

台北市 10422 信義路三段
59 號 11 樓
永安有限公司人事經理
費伊凡先生收

親愛的費先生：

我相信我的教育、訓練及個人條件使我具備了貴公司五月二十七日
在中國時報徵求執行助理一職廣告所要求的背景。

七年未間斷的的祕書工作經驗裏，其中五年在外商公司，教我如何
處理各方面的辦公室事務。由於所在公司的職員很少，我要執行許
多不同的任務。我會打字、處理文件、信函、操作電話及當招待員。

我相信我的個性能使我適合貴公司。我喜歡人而且經由經驗我學會
了如何與人共事。我樂於接受一個能提供給我變化、新任務和責任
的工作挑戰。

附帶的簡歷詳述了我的背景，我可否在您方便的時間會見您，討論
工作的可能性？請撥 281-1882 找我。

周曉琪　敬上

The Cover Letter

3rd Fl., 142,
Chang-an E. Rd., Sec. 2,
Taipei 10629

May 26, 2008

Mr. Robert Ford
Director, Personnel Department
Atlantic Taiwan Corporation
5th Fl., 3, Lane 79,
Fuhsing S. Rd, Sec. 1,
Taipei 10717

Dear Mr. Ford:

With my ten years experience as administrative assistant
and executive secretary of a small-scale foreign capital
company, I would like to apply for the position of
executive secretary which you advertised in the United
Daily News of May 24.

I have been directly responsible to Mr. Robert Hailey,
president of Stanford Taiwan for the past three years.
In addition to the usual secretarial work, I am
responsible for screening his telephone calls and
visitors, scheduling all of his appointments, and
organizing his paperwork and correspondence.

Practically, I do everything I can to make his heavy
work easier, so, I am familiar with the responsibilities
of an executive secretary. I believe that responsible
business experience, expertise in secretarial skills
and procedures, and a sincere desire to work in the
field of executive secretary qualify me for the
position.

** screen〔skrin〕*v.* 篩選

expertise〔ˌɛkspɚ'tiz〕*n.* 專業知識和技術

附函英漢對照

台北市 10629 長安東路
二段 142 號 3 樓

2008 年 5 月 26 日

台北市 10717 復興南路一段
79 巷 3 號 5 樓
太平洋台灣公司人事主任
羅勃特福特先生

親愛的福特先生：

以我在一家小規範外資公司十年行政助理和執行祕書的經驗，我
想應徵貴公司登在五月二十四日聯合報所徵求的執行祕書一職。

我在過去三年直接對史丹福台灣公司的董事長羅勃特海利先生負責。
除了一般的祕書工作，我還負責篩選他的電話及訪客、安排約會時
間表、處理文件及信函。

事實上，我盡我所能減輕他繁重的工作，所以，我很熟悉執行祕書
的職責。我相信可靠的事務經驗、對祕書技巧及程序的事業知識以
及懇切想在執行祕書的領域上工作，可使我勝任此職位。

I have two children, but my mother lives with me and takes good care of them; so, I can devote myself to the new environment. I like working with people so I feel confident, too, that I can adjust smoothly to the transition from a small firm to a large organization.

I would be happy to come for an interview at your convenience to discuss my qualifications in person. I can be reached at 5917133 after 7 p.m. any weekday.

Sincerely yours,

Milly Yeh

【 附函首段範例 】:

I'll be graduating this summer with a degree in English Department from Fu Jen Catholic University and will be seeking employment with firms which deal with English speaking clients. I am aware of your company's reputation for professionalism and would very much like to join your highly competent bilingual staff.

✻   ✻   ✻

I'll be finishing my military service this winter. As an infantry officer I am experienced in motivating men under the most difficult situations. I am thus confident in my ability to deal with people. The key to success in any organization is motivating its people to give their best. In this mission I feel well prepared to join your management team.

我有兩個小孩，但母親與我同住並妥善照料他們；所以我可以全心投入新的環境。我喜歡與人一起工作所以我也自信能順利地適應由小公司轉到大機構的轉變。

我樂意在您方便的時候與您面談，親自討論我的資格。您可在星期一至星期六晚上七點後電 5917133 找我。

葉蜜莉　敬上

【要點提示】：對一個即將畢業，就要踏入社會的人來說，謙虛而誠懇的態度不僅重要，也必須道出自己的專長及目標讓人一目瞭然。

我今年夏天將自輔仁大學獲英文系學士學位畢業，正欲尋求公司與英語說講客戶打交道的工作。我知道貴公司以從事專門職業稱譽，非常想加入貴公司雙語能力很好的職員陣容中。

※　　　　　※　　　　　※

我今年冬天將服完兵役。身為一個步兵軍官，我有經驗在最困難的狀況下推動人。因此有自信可以和人相處。任何機構成功的關鍵在於激發人員盡其所能。在這任務上，我覺得已準備好加入貴公司的管理隊伍。

The Cover Letter

2F, 85 Chung Shan
N. Rd., Sec. 2,
Taipei 10413

September 8, 2008

Ms. Constance Rohatyn
Great Wall Securities Inc.
170 Nanking E. Rd., Sec. 4,
Taipei

Dear Ms. Rohatyn:

I'm writing to apply for the position of an account executive trainee in your firm. I have just graduated recently this summer from Soochow University. Through my father I have learned a great deal about the securities business, himself a stockbroker. In my years in college, I realized that this was the line of work that interest me the most.

While in college, I participated in a lot of activities both on the collegiate level and the departmental level. I attended a lot of symposia and conferences on the business of stockbroking. When I had the chance I also visited some firms for my practicum. I mention this because I know that my line of work is a demanding one and I'm willing to show that I can face up to any challenge placed before me.

Could we talk more on my prospects of joining your firm? I'll be free any day of the week for an interview with you. You'll find my resume attached with this letter. I will appreciate it if you can give me a reply as soon as you can. Until then, I remain.

Sincerely yours,

Dar-tian Hong

＊＊ security〔sɪˊkjʊrətɪ〕*n.* 證券；股票　symposia〔sɪmˊpozɪə〕*n.* 座談會
practicum〔ˊpræktəkəm〕*n.* 大學的實驗或實習課程
face up to sth 誠實而又勇敢的承認和對付

附函英漢對照

台北市 10413 中山北路
二段 85 號 2 樓

2008 年 9 月 8 日

台北市南京東路四段 170 號
偉城證券公司
康絲坦絲洛哈台小姐

親愛的洛哈台小姐：

　　我寫這封信想應徵貴公司會計執行見習生的職位。我今年夏天才剛自東吳大學畢業。由於我的父親，我學了很多關於證券的買賣交易，他是一個證券經紀人。大學時，我就明白了這是讓我最感興趣的工作事業。

　　大學的時候，我參加很多活動，有學院級也有學系級的。我也參加很多以股票買賣交易為題的座談會和會議。有機會時，我還為我的實習課程參觀了一些公司。我提到這件事因為我知道這份職業是一份要求嚴苛的工作，而我願表現出我能勇敢地對付置於我之前的挑戰。

　　我們能談更多我加入貴公司的遠景嗎？我星期中的任何一天都有空與您面談。您會發現我隨此信附寄的履歷表。如果您能儘快地給我答覆，我將很感激。靜候回音。

洪達天　敬上

The Cover Letter

56, Lane 47,
Chu-lin Rd., Yung-ho,
Taipei County 20237

July 7, 2008

Ms. Miles Skeat
Administrative Department
Hua-mei, Ltd.
4th Fl., 78,
Chung-shan N. Rd., Sec. 1,
Taipei 10555

Dear Ms. Skeat:

　　I have learned from the advertisement in the United Daily News of July 6 that you are looking for a staff member for your accounting department. With thorough college education in accounting and related studies, various bookkeeping experiences, and strong interest in this field, I feel I can be considered for the position.

　　The accounting courses I took at the university include up-to-date procedures. Courses in computer science have led me to be especially interested in EDP accounting. These courses provided information useful for working with computers which, I understand, is essential in your organization.

　　As the enclosed resume shows, I found it necessary to work while completing my education, and, consequently, I have learned to apportion my time and, at the same time, I have developed effective communication and human relations skills, which would be assests in working in an intercultural environment.

** asset〔'æsɛt〕 n. 有價值或有用的東西

**附函英漢對照**

台北縣 20237 永和市竹
林路 47 巷 56 號

2008 年 7 月 7 日

台北市 10555 中山北路
一段 78 號 4 樓
華美有限公司行政部門
麥爾斯史基特女士

親愛的史基特女士：

　　我從七月六日聯合報的廣告中得知貴公司會計部在徵求職員。由於大學裏會計及其它相關科目、充分的訓練、不同的簿記經驗及對此科強烈的興趣，我覺得可以被列為此職位的考慮人選。

　　我在大學修的會計課程包括最新式的程序。電腦課程使我對電子資料處理會計特別有興趣。這些課程提供操作電腦時的有用資料；我知道，電腦在貴機構是不可缺少的。

　　就如所附簡歷所言，在我完成學業時發覺工作的必要，因此，我學會分配時間，同時培養了有效的溝通和人際關係技巧，這對在不同文化環境中工作將有助益。

By referring to the enclosed resume, you will be
able to form a more complete idea of my background. May
I discuss further with you my qualifications for the
position of accountant in your organization? I would
appreciate your call at 9246279 to name a time when I
may come, at your convenience.

Sincerely yours,

Maureen Shao

【 附函正文範例 】：

The advertisement specified experience and English
fluency as vital. I've gained valuable work experience
and perfected my English by studying and working in the
United States. I have a PhD from the University of
Illinois in electrical engineering and was employed by
Apple Computer for 5 years. My primary reason for
leaving Apple Computer is because I wanted to return
to Taiwan.

In response to your ad for a tour group leader I
would like to point out my personal experiences with
traveling. I have traveled throughout Europe and South
America on my own. The problems I've encountered and
overcome have taught me a lot, whether it's sickness,
language problems, or culture shock. As a tour leader
my personal experiences will help me handle some of
the hazards which my tour group will face.

　　參考附寄的簡歷表，您將能對我的背景有更完整的概念。我可否進一步與您討論我擔任貴機構會計員的資格？如蒙來電 9246279 指定一個您方便的時間會面，將不勝感激。

　　　　　　　　　　　　　　　　邵穆林　敬上

【要點提示】：附函的正文中提到自己所具備的資格和能力，並強調出經歷和學歷，將是一項說服雇主的有力證據。

　　廣告中載明經驗和流利的英語是不可或缺的。在美國工作和讀書期間，我獲得了寶貴的工作經驗，並增進我的英文。我拿到伊利諾大學電機工程的博士學位，並受雇於蘋果電腦公司五年。離開蘋果電腦公司的首要理由是我想回來台灣。

　　回覆貴公司廣告徵求旅行團領隊，我想指出我旅行的個人經驗。我自己遊遍歐洲和南美。我所碰到及解決的問題使我學了很久，不論是疾病、語言問題、或是文化衝擊。作為一名真正的領隊，我個人的經驗會幫助我處理我的旅行團會碰到的一些危險。

The Cover Letter

3rd Fl., 17,
Ho-ping E. Rd., Sec. 2,
Taipei 10311

May 13, 2008

Mr. Keith Sanger
Personnel Department
Marion Far East, Co., Ltd.
12th Fl., 126,
Tun-hua N. Rd.,
Taipei 10414

Dear Mr. Sanger:

With my diversified work experience and my college education in accounting, I feel I am qualified to apply for the accounting position with your firm. Your advertisement of May 12 in the China Times News calls for an individual with accounting skills and a desire to work into a management position. This description matches me exactly.

During my studies at the university, accounting was my special field of interest. I completed courses of accounting with high grades, and EDP accounting became one of the most interesting subjects for me.

During my career at Dafa Trading I have performed various aspects of accounting procedures, and while working in the New York office, I gained valuable experience and knowledge of American-style accounting procedures.

My resume will give you additional information about my interests and background.

I should welcome the opportunity of meeting with you at your convenience. Please let me know when we can get together to talk further about a career with Marion Far East. You can reach me at my home after 7 p.m. at 5413723.

Sincerely yours,

Ivy Chuang

附函英漢對照

台北市 10311 和平東路
二段 17 號 3 樓
2008 年 5 月 13 日

台北市 10414 敦化北路
126 號 12 樓
瑪瑞安遠東有限公司人事室
契斯桑格先生

親愛的桑格先生：

由於我有不同的工作經驗並在大學接受會計學教育，我覺得我有資格應徵貴公司的會計工作。貴公司五月十二日在中國時報廣告徵求一個有會計技能並想從事管理工作的人，這敍述正好適合我。

在大學求學時期，會計是我特別感興趣的一科，我以高分修完會計，以外，電子資料處理會計也成爲我最感興趣的科目之一。

在大發貿易公司工作的期間，我完成了許多不同方面的會計程序，而且我在紐約分公司工作期間，得到有關美式會計程序方面可貴的經驗及知識。

我的簡歷將提供給您有關我的興趣及背景的額外資料。

我很樂意有機會在您方便的時候與您會面。請通知我我們何時可以見面進一步討論在瑪瑞安遠東公司的工作。您可在晚間七點後打電話 5413723 到我家找我。

莊愛薇　敬上

The Cover Letter

59 Sinyi Road, Sec. 2,
Taipei.

April 10, 2008

Mr. Su
General Manager
World Seas Trading Co., Ltd.
12 Fushin S. Rd.,
Taipei

Dear Mr. Su:

I'm writing in reply to your request through the University Placement Center for a business assistant in your company. I will graduate this coming summer. My outstanding record at school and some experience in business has prepared me for the tasks in the work you are calling for.

I am really interested in learning the practical side of business, and also a diligent worker and a fast learner. If given a chance, I am sure I can prove my worth in your company.

I will be available during the weekdays in the morning for any interviews you may want to give. Enclosed is my resume and some letters of recommendations from my teachers in the university. Hoping for your immediate reply.

Sincerely yours,

Marie Chao

enc.

** placement〔ˊplesmənt〕 *n.* 工作介紹

附函英漢對照

台北市信義路二段 59 號

2008 年 4 月 10 日

台北市復興南路 12 號
世界海運貿易有限公司
總經理
蘇先生

親愛的蘇先生：

　　我寫信回覆貴公司透過大學工作介紹中心徵求的一名業務助理。我在這個夏天就要畢業了。在學校突出的記錄和在商業上某些經驗，已使我準備好去作你所要求的工作上的任務。

　　我真的有興趣去學習商業實務的一面，同時也是一個勤勉的工作者和學習很快的人。如果能有機會，我確信我可以證明在貴公司的價值。

　　週一到週六上午您想和我面談，我都可以。附上我的履歷表和大學老師的幾封推薦函。希望很快有您的回音。

趙美莉　敬上

有附件

The Cover Letter

49 5F Lane 37,
Keelung Rd., Sec. 2,
Taipei 10264

January 30, 2009

Mr. Greg Reilly,
Personnel Manager
Horng Yeou Department Store
98 Chunghsiao E. Rd.
Sec. 3,
Taipei

Dear Mr. Reilly:

I'm interested in applying for the position of assistant merchandiser you advertised in the United Daily News of January 15, I believe I have the necessary qualities that you are looking for. Aside from my professional qualifications, personally I enjoy the type of work I am doing right now. I like to travel, do negotiation work and meet all sorts of people.

I'm sure that I can be a valued addition to your firm. Besides my knowledge of the business and the market and my professional and personal background, I am quite confident that I can do well the job you are offering.

I'd be willing to set an appointment with you any day at your convenience. You'll find my resume attached here. My telephone number and address are indicated therein, I'd appreciate it very much if you can give me a call or write to me as soon as you can.

Sincerely,

Jaan-chuan Lee

台北市 10264 基隆路
37 巷 49 號 5 樓
2009 年 1 月 30 日

台北市忠孝東路三段 98 號
宏有百貨公司人事經理
格雷格雷利先生

親愛的雷利先生：

　　我對於應徵貴公司刊登在 1 月 15 日聯合報上的採購助理一職很感興趣。我相信我具備了貴公司所希望的資格。除了我的專業資格之外，我個人很喜歡我現在所從事的工作型態。我喜歡旅行，作談判的工作，以及接觸各式各樣的人。

　　我確信可以成為貴公司新增重要的一員。除了我商業和市場貿易的知識以及專業和個人的背景外，我相當自信能做好貴公司所提供的工作。

　　我很樂意在任何一天方便時訂個約定會面的時間。您將可以看到附寄的履歷表。我的電話號碼以及住址就在裏頭，如果您能儘快打電話給我或寫信給我，將不勝感激。

　　　　　　　　　　　　　　　　　李展川　敬上

 **The Cover Letter**

4F, 45 Wen Chou St.,
Taipei 10253

May 9, 2008

Mr. Stuart Malone
Director of Personnel
Columbia Inc., Taipei Branch
80, Nanking E. Rd., Sec. 4,
Taipei

Dear Mr. Malone:

I am replying to your advertisement in the United Daily News of May 2 for a Marketing Assistant in your Sales Department.

My courses at Tung Hai University were specially planned to prepare me for a career in marketing. My studies, I feel, have given me the foundation of knowledge from which to learn the practical side of marketing.

In my capacity as the executive promotion manager assistant of Rockwelle Industrial Concerns Inc., I have had a very extensive training in my field. This practical experience has exposed me to the real nature of business today. With this stint at Rockwelle I became more interested in the world of marketing more than ever.

I have had a very good job at Rockwelle but I feel that I have to move on to learn more things in a growing company. I'm sure that I will be able to contribute more in such working conditions. The enclosed resume shows details of my background which, I believe, will qualify me as a member of your sales force.

If you need to know more about me or need to clarify anything in my resume, you can reach me at this number 3217359 after 8 p.m. any weekday.

Sincerely yours,

Ho-Chung Chan

附函英漢對照

台北市 10253 溫州街
45 號 4 樓

2008 年 5 月 9 日

台北市南京東路四段 80 號
哥倫比亞台北分公司人事主任
史道馬龍先生

親愛的馬龍先生：

我要回覆貴公司五月二日在聯合報的廣告，徵求一位行銷部門的市場銷售助理。

我在東海大學的課程是特別爲我在市場買賣方面的事業而設計準備的。我覺得我的課程已給了我基本的知識，並且從中學習到市場貿易實務的一面。

作爲洛克斐勒工業股份公司執行推廣經理助理的能力，在我的領域裏我有非常廣泛的訓練。這種實際的經驗讓我接觸到今天商業的眞正性質。由於在洛克斐勒這份指定的工作，我比以往更對市場貿易方面感到興趣。

我在洛克斐勒公司一直有不錯的工作，但我覺得我必須換到一家成長中的公司繼續學更多的事情。我確信我可以貢獻更多於如是的工作狀況。附寄的履歷表可看出我的背景細節，我相信將使我有資格成爲銷售力量之一。

如果您需要知道更多有關我的事情，或需要澄清我履歷表中的任何事情，您可以在週一至週六晚上八點之後，撥 3217359 找我。

張和忠　敬上

The Cover Letter

59 3F Roosevelt Road
Sec. 3,
Taipei 10021
April 26, 2008

Miss Ian Chi
Ming-Yang Corporation
157, Ho-ping W. Rd.,
Sec. 3,
Taipei

Dear Ms. Chi:

I am replying to your advertisement in the China Times News of April 15 for a staff member in your international sales department. With my educational background, I believe, I am qualified for the position.

The world of international business has been of great interest for me, as you can see in the courses I have taken in my college. Not mentioned though in my resume is the fact that I enjoy challenges and working with other people. I am also very hard working and resolute in the goals that I pursue.

I would very much want to set an appointment with you regarding my qualifications in relation to your requirements. You can write me at the above address or call me at 3415813 any weekday after 8 p.m.

Sincerely Yours,

Huey-Chyi; Wang

** resolute〔ˈrɛzəˌlut, ˈrɛzḷ/jut〕adj. 堅決的；斷然的

附函英漢對照

台北市 10021 羅斯福路
三段 59 號 3 樓

2008 年 4 月 26 日

台北市和平西路三段
157 號
名揚公司
季怡安小姐

親愛的季小姐：

我是回覆貴公司四月十五日在中國時報的廣告，徵求國際行銷部門的一名職員，以我的學歷背景，我相信使我有資格擔任這個職位。

國際商務的領域一直是我相當感興趣的，正如你可見到我在大學時所修的科目。雖然在我的履歷表中沒有提到，事實上我非常喜歡挑戰，以及和別人一起工作。同時我非常努力工作，在我追求的目標上也很堅決。

關於我的資格和貴公司要求相關的地方，我非常希望能和您訂個會面的時間，您可以寫信到上述地址給我，或者週一至週六晚上八點之後撥 3415813 找我。

王慧琪　敬上

The Cover Letter

6th Fl., 852
Ming-Sheng E. Rd.,
Taipei 10200

June 24, 2008

Ms. Ian Chi
Ming-Yang Corporation
157, Ho-ping W. Rd., Sec. 3,
Taipei 10714

Dear Ms. Chi:

I am replying to your advertisement in the China Times
News of June 23 for an experienced staff member in
your foreign trade department. With my educational
background and work experience, I believe, I am well
qualified for the position.

My major field of study at university was internationl
marketing, with emphasis on foreign trade practice and
English business communication. In addition, I have
been working for the past eight years with Far East
Trading Co. where my responsibilities have included
shipping arrangements, forign exchange procedures, and
some business transactions in import and export of
synthetic textiles.

Each year, new responsibilities were assigned to me
and I have been involved in various aspects of foreign
trade and at the same time learned how important it is
for all sections to work together. I enjoy working with
people, tackling challenges and accepting responsibilities.

** transaction〔træns'ækʃən, trænz'ækʃən〕*n*. 處理
　 assign〔ə'saɪn〕*v*. 分派；指派　aspect〔'æspɛkt〕*n*. 觀點；方面
　 tackle〔'tækl〕*v*. 處理；應付

附函英漢對照

台北市 10200 民生東路
852 號 6 樓

2008 年 6 月 24 日

台北市 10714 和平西路
三段 157 號
名揚公司
季怡安小姐

親愛的季小姐：

我想回覆貴公司六月二十三日在中國時報徵求有經驗的外貿部職員的廣告。以我的教育背景及工作經驗，我相信我能勝任這個工作。

我在大學主修的是國際市場，著重於外貿實務及英語商務溝通。此外，我過去八年在遠東貿易公司工作，職責包括安排裝貨、外滙程序及一些人工織物的進出口業務處理。

每年都有新的任務指派給我，我也從事過許多不同方面的外貿工作，同時知道各部門一起運作的重要性。我喜歡與人共事、迎接挑戰、及承擔責任。

My resume is enclosed, but I would welcome the opportunity of meeting with you personally to discuss my
qualifications as they relate to your requirements.
Will you please write me at the above address or call
me at 7622413 any weekday after 8 p.m.

　　　　　　　　　　　　　　　　　　Sincerely yours,

　　　　　　　　　　　　　　　　　　Molly Su

【附函正文範例】：

　　If I may elaborate on my resume, I hired
initially as a typist for a trading company's accounting department but became an accountant when the
supervisor realized I had a knack for numbers. I
learned accounting on the job and have never studied
it formally. In addition, I've taught myself to be
proficient with WORDSTAR and TELEX.

　　　　　　　�֍　　　　　　✖　　　　　✖

　　If I may speak on some of my personal qualities,
I am loyal, hard-working, and have the ability to get
along with all kinds of people. I enjoy challenging
work and thrive under pressure. Furthermore I am not
afraid of responsibilities. I seek a tough job. Where
others fail, I will succeed.

隨信附寄我的簡歷，但我更樂意有機會親自與您會面討論我的資格，因為那和貴公司的要求有關，請寫信至上述地址或於星期一至星期六晚上八點以後電 7622413 。

蘇茉莉 敬上

【要點提示】：附函正文中提到自己勤奮向學、無師自通，正好補充了履歷表中有限的說明，是附函正文中的重點所在。

容我就我的履歷表詳細說明，我最初受雇為一家貿易公司會計部門的一名打字員，但是當管理者明白我有數字的竅門，便成了會計。我在工作中學得了會計，從來不曾正式的學過。除此之外，我無師自通了WORDSTAR和TELEX 。

    ❀   ❀   ❀

容我說一些我個人的特質，我忠誠、勤奮，並有能力與各式各樣的人相處。我喜歡有挑戰性的工作，在壓力之下更能發展，並且不怕擔負職責。我謀求一份困難的工作。別人無法作到的，我會完成。

The Cover Letter

8th Fl., 3 Hsin Hai Road,
Sec. 3, Taipei 10233

February 1, 2008

Mr. Craig Hoffman
Leighton & Brinkley, Inc.
18th Fl., 3, 78 Chungking
S. Rd., Taipei

Dear Mr. Hoffman:

    I'm applying for any position in your personnel department. If you have a job opening now or maybe later in the future, please consider me as a condidate for the job.

    I believe I could do well in a company like yours. Although I have just graduated and still don't have any practical experience in my chosen field of vocation, my past experiences and educational background I'm confident has given me the right qualifications for the job. While working at Taiwan Television Enterprise Ltd., I was able to meet various kinds of people and experiences. This was my first practical experience of working as a wage-earner. In this working environment the value of a team spirit has not been lost on me. Dedication to one's work is also one thing that I have learned from my co-workers and superiors.

    Please keep me in mind when a vacancy in your company becomes available. I would appreciate it if we could set an appointment so you can get to know me better. My resume is enclosed with this letter. Thank you for your kind attention. I hope to hear from you soon.

                Yours sincerely,

                Bih-Yeu Chang

** *wage-earner* 工資勞動者   *be lost upon sb* 未能影響或引起注意

附函英漢對照

台北市 10233 辛亥路
三段 3 號 8 樓

2008 年 2 月 1 日

台北市重慶南路
78 號 18 樓之 3
雷頓布林克利公司
克雷格霍夫曼 先生

親愛的霍夫曼先生：

　　我想應徵貴公司人事部門的任何職位。如果貴公司有空缺的工作，或是將來可能會有的，請考慮我為這個職位的候選人。

　　我相信我可以在像貴公司這樣的公司做的很好。雖然在我才剛畢業並且在選擇行業的領域裏，我仍沒有任何的實務經驗，我自信過去的經歷和學歷背景能給予我這份工作最合適的資格。在台灣電視公司工作時，我得以碰見各種不同的人和經驗。這是我第一次作為工資勞動者的實務經驗。在這個工作環境裏，團隊精神的價值已引起我的注意。奉獻於工作上也是我從我的工作夥伴及上司處學到的一件事情。

　　當貴公司有職缺時，請記得我。如果我們能訂個會面的時間我會很感激，您也可以對我更瞭解。隨信附寄我的履歷表。謝謝您的關照，希望能很快得到您的回訊。

張碧瑜　敬上

The Cover Letter

2nd Fl., 38, Alley 12
Lane 182, Roosevelt Rd.,
Sec. 3, Taipei 10319

June 11, 2008

Mr. Stuard Malone
Director of Personnel
Maxwell Taipei Branch
80, Chung-hsiao E. Rd.,
Sec. 4, Taipei 10222

Dear Mr. Malone:

I am replying to your advertisement in the United
Daily News of June 10 for a managerial staff member in
your personnel department.

My courses at Taiwan University were specially planned
to prepare me for a career in personnel management. My
studies, I feel, have given me the foundation of
knowledge from which to learn the practical side of
personnel management.

At Taiwan Hamilton Co. I have conducted extensive
interviews to clarify the way employees perceive their
roles, concerns and priorities. This practical experience has given me a more complete understanding of the
importance of good human relations. It also inspired
me to further develop my skills in personnel management.

** foundation〔faʊnˈdeʃən〕n. 基礎；根據
   conduct〔kənˈdʌkt〕v. 管理；經營
   clarify〔ˈklærəˌfaɪ〕v. 明瞭

附函英漢對照

台北市 10319 羅斯福路三段
182 巷 12 弄 38 號 2 樓

2008 年 6 月 11 日

台北市 10222 忠孝東路
四段 80 號
麥斯威爾台北分公司人事主任
史都華馬倫先生

親愛的馬倫先生：

我想回覆貴公司六月十日在聯合報所登徵求人事部管理人員的廣告。

我在台灣大學的課程特別是為了替我的人事管理事業鋪路而設計的，我認為我的學業給予我學習實際人事管理的基本知識。

在台灣漢明頓公司，我曾經作過許多訪談，去了解員工怎麼理解他們的角色、關心的東西及事情的優先程度。這個實際經驗使我對良好人際關係的重要性有更完整的了解，同時激發我進一步發展我的人事管理技巧。

I have been very happy with my work at Taiwan Hamilton
Co. but I am anxious to assume broader responsibilities
in a growing company. The enclosed resume shows details
of my background which, I believe, qualifies me to be
a successful member of your managerial staff in your
personnel department.

May I have an opportunity of talking with you in person
to tell you more about my desire to work in your
organization? Self-addressed postcard is enclosed, but
if you perfer to call me, you may reach me at **3416923,**
after **8** p.m. any weekday.

Sincerely yours,

Tessa Mo

【 附函結尾範例 】：

    Enclosed are my resume and letters of recommenda-
tion. I am eager to begin work immediately and my only
requirevent is a minimum salary of N.T.$15,000. I am
confident that you'll be happy with my work. Please
contact me at your earliest convenience. I can be
reached at **713-5428.**

我很滿意在台灣漢明頓公司的工作，但我渴望能在一家成長中的公司承擔更大的責任。附寄的簡歷詳述我的背景，我相信這些應該可使我有資格成為貴公司人事管理部成功的一員。

我可否有機會親自與您談更多有關我想在貴機構工作的願望？隨信附寄有住址的明信片，但如果您較願意打電話給我，請於週一至週六晚間八點後來電 3416923 。

莫黛莎　敬上

【要點提示】：在附函的結尾可以提出自己的希望待遇，並表示出
　　　　　　　希望能早日有回音，能再一次提到自己的電話號碼
　　　　　　　也很恰當。

　　附上我的履歷表和推薦函。我非常希望能馬上開始工作，而唯一的要求是最低薪資一萬五千元，我很有信心你將會對我的工作感到滿意。請在方便時儘早和我聯絡。可以打 713-5428 聯絡到我。

The Cover Letter

3rd Fl., 83, Lane 212
Chi-lin Rd.,
Taiwpi 10237
July 22, 2008

Mr. Kevin Kendall
Personnel Manager
Summit Corporation
6th Fl., 147, Hsinyi Rd., Sec 3,
Taipei 10633

Dear Mr. Kendall:

Please consider me for the position of computer programmer that you advertised in the China Times News of July 21.

For the past three years, I have been working as a computer programmer for Computer World Co. and in this work I have operated a YBM-TX computer.

In addition to the work experience, I have an educational background with a major in computer science, including programming, systems design and analysis, and operating systems. I have completed advanced courses in FORTRAN and PASCAL languages.

My work experience, together with educational preparation, as shown on the enclosed resume, would qualify me for the position. I have a strong desire to pursue my career in computer programming in the environment of a foreign capital company.

May I have the priviledge of an interview to discuss my qualifications with you in detail? I would appreciate it if you would write or call me at 5926403 to set up an appointment.

Sincerely yours,

Vernon Chang

** pursue〔pə'su, -'sɪu〕v. 繼續   capital〔'kæpətḷ〕n. 資金；資本

附函英漢對照

台北市 10237 吉林路
212 巷 83 號 3 樓

2008 年 7 月 22 日

台北市 10633 信義路
三段 147 號 6 樓
舒美公司人事經理
凱文甘德爾先生

親愛的甘德爾先生：

　　請考慮用我為貴公司七月二十一日在中國時報廣告徵求的電腦程式設計師。

　　過去三年，我在電腦世界公司做程式設計員，並在這工作裏操縱一部 YBM - TX 電腦。

　　除了這個工作經驗以外，我還有主修電腦的教育背景，包括程式設計，系統設計、分析及作業系統。我還完成了 FORTRAN 和 PASCAL 語言的高級課程。

　　我的工作經驗，加上我教育方面的準備，如附寄的簡歷所述，應能使我勝任這個工作。我有強烈的慾望，想在外資公司的環境下繼續我的電腦程式設計事業。

　　我可不可以有這個權利與您會面詳細討論我的資格？如蒙來信或來電 5926403 安排會面，將不勝感激。

張維能　敬上

The Cover Letter

10 Minchuan E. Rd.
Taipei 10376

November 4, 2008

Mr. Allen Mayo,
General Manager
Chico Computers Mfg. Inc.
4 FL., 36 Chung Yang Road,
Taipei

Dear Mr. Mayo:

I'm writing in response to an ad that you placed in today's papers. I'm sure I can contribute a lot to a growing company like yours.

I have had more than ten years of experience in the computer service business. Although I am a woman, in which unfortunately is a man's world, you can count on me on doing a good job. This is proven by my rising to the supervisory level in my present job.

I feel that I have the qualifications that you are calling for. May I see you to discuss further my application to your company. Enclosed you'll find my resume. Please give me a call at 712-3876 at your earliest possible time to set an appointment. Thank you very much.

Sincerely yours,

Yang Lih-jeng

台北市 10376 民權東路
10 號

2008 年 11 月 4 日

台北市重陽路 36 號 4 樓
智高電腦製造公司
總經理　艾倫馬又先生

親愛的馬又先生：

　　我寫信回覆貴公司在今天報紙上所刊登的廣告。我確信我可以在一個像貴公司這樣成長中的公司裏貢獻良多。

　　我在電腦服務事務方面已有超過十年的經驗。雖然我是女的，很不幸地卻是個男人的世界，但你可以信任我能做好工作，這可以由我在現職工作晉升到管理階層得到證明。

　　我覺得我有貴公司所要求的資格。我可以見您，來談談更多關於我申請加入貴公司的事嗎？您可以見到我附寄的履歷表。請儘可能很快打 712-3876 給我，約定一個會面的時間。非常謝謝您。

楊麗珍　敬上

The Cover Letter

5F, No. 19 Lane 390
Tun Hwa S. Road,
Taipei 10623

October 10, 2008

Mr. Ivan Philippe
Personnel Manager
Sun Valley Enterprises Ltd.,
11th Fl., 59 Hsinyi Rd.,
Sec. 3, Taipei

Dear Mr. Philippe:

I believe my education, training and personal qualities give the background you desire for the position of electrical engineer you advertised in the China Times News of October 5.

My three years of continuous experience in my career has taught me how to deal with all phases of the business I'm in right now. Because of the rather small staff of the company I worked for, I dealt not only in the responsibilities of my job but also in the various aspects of the business, I'm familiar with office procedures, and have established a wide range of contacts in the business of building construction.

I'm a very independent and motivated worker. Furthermore I am very systematic and thorough with my work. I pay a lot of attention to details without sacrificing speed efficiency and costs.

I believe that I have the personal qualities that would fit me in harmoniously with your firm. Enclosed is my resume. Please feel free to call me any time you want to discuss my possibility of joining your firm. My number is 7715115.

Sincerely yours,

David Lang

＊＊ systematic〔ˌsɪstə'mætɪk〕 *adj.* 有系統的
　　thorough〔'θɝo, -ə〕 *adj.* 徹底的；認眞的

附函英漢對照

台北市 10623 敦化南路
390 巷 19 號 5 樓
2008 年 10 月 10 日

台北市信義路三段 59 號 11 樓
太陽谷有限公司人事經理
伊凡菲利浦先生

親愛的菲利浦先生：

我相信我的教育、訓練、個人特質，能給予貴公司在十月五日中國時報所刊登電機工程師一職所需要的背景。

在我事業上三年不斷的經驗教我如何處理我現在所從事職務的所有層面。由於我所服務的公司職員很少，我不僅要處理我工作上的職責，同時也有不同方面的事務。我很熟悉辦公室的程序，並已和房屋建造生意建立起廣大範圍的連繫。

我是個非常獨立且積極的工作者。另外在工作上，非常有系統而且認真。我相當注意細節，不會犧牲速率和成本。

我相信我有此種特質，能讓我在貴公司非常的適應。附上我的履歷表。您想和我討論加入貴公司的可能性時，請隨意在任何時間打電話給我。號碼是 7715115。

藍大僑 敬上

The Cover Letter

95 Tung Hwa St.,
Lane 34,
Taipei 10653
March 22, 2008

Mr. Keith Sanger
Personnel Department
Far East Development Co., Ltd.
12th Fl., 125
Tung Hwa N. Rd.,
Taipei

Dear Mr. Sanger:

I am writing in response to an ad you have placed in China Times News on March 18. I believe I have the necessary qualifications that you have called for in the position of Designs Engineer in your company.

Besides my nine years of experience for the present company that I'm working for, you'll also find it to your satisfaction that my years in college has grounded me in the necessary skills and knowledge in the field where I can safely say that I can now do well in.

I will very much like to have the opportunity to meet you to discuss further anything pertinent to my qualifications. You can reach me at the above address or call me at this number 7023141 in the evenings any day from 8 p.m. onwards. I am looking forward to hearing from you soon.

Sincerely yours,

Chau-jye Yih

** *call for* 要求；需求　　ground〔graʊnd〕 *v.* 打基礎
to one's satisfaction 使某人滿意　　pertinent〔'pɝtn̩ənt〕 *adj.* 有關係的
onwards〔'ɑnwɚdz〕 *adv.* 向前；前進

台北市 10653 通化街
34 巷 95 號
2008 年 3 月 22 日

台北市敦化南路 125 號 12 樓
遠東發展有限公司
人事部門　凱斯桑格先生

親愛的桑格先生：

　　我在回覆貴公司在三月十八日的中國時報上所刊登的廣告。我相信我有貴公司設計工程師一職所要求的必備資格。

　　除了我在現在的公司工作了九年的經驗外，你同時會發現你會很滿意，我在大學時已為我在這領域所必備的技能和知識打下了基礎，我可以很確定地說我現在做得很好。

　　我非常希望能有機會見您，討論更多和我的資格有關的事情。你可以寫信到上述地址給我，或者每天晚上八點以後撥 7023141 找我。希望很快收到您的消息。

易超傑　敬上

**The
Cover
Letter**

3F No. 158 Yenchi St.,
Taipei 10212

August 9, 2008

Mr. Craig Lansing
Concourse Magazine, Co.
12, Jen Ai Road, Sec. 3,
Taipei

Dear Mr. Lansing:

I have had the experience in working in the world
of publishing. Although I am not a professional writer,
I have had the chance to do some writing on the side in
the course of working for my employers and in my summer
vacations in college. My writings have been well received by the readers of our publication and the community I worked for.

I saw your advertisement for a freelance writer
for your magazine and through the encouragement of one
of your staff, Mrs. Sung, I wish to apply for the vacant
position in your organization. I understand that this
will be on a per assignment basis. I'm quite willing to
work under these conditions while I am still working in
my present job. I assure you though that there won't be
any conflict of interest.

I've enclosed my resume with this letter and a
sample of my work. I can come for an interview with you
any day of the week but please give me a 2 day notice
so I can make the proper arrangements. Should you have
any questions or wish to contact me, my address and
telephone number is written on my resume.

Sincerely yours,

Jean Chiou

** *in the course of* 在…期間

**附函英漢對照**

台北市 10212 延吉街
158 號 3 樓
2008 年 8 月 9 日

台北市仁愛路三段 12 號
滙流雜誌公司
克雷格蘭辛先生

親愛的蘭辛先生：

　　我曾經有出版方面工作的經驗。雖然我不是專業的作家，在我為我的老闆及大學暑假的工作期間，我有機會在這方面作些寫作。我所寫的東西曾為我們出版刊物及我所工作的社區的讀者徹底接受。

　　我看到了貴雜誌徵求一名自由作家的廣告，並經由貴公司職員孫女士的鼓勵，我希望應徵貴機構這份空缺的職位。我明白這是按件分派的方式。我非常願意當我仍在做目前的工作時，在這種情況下工作。我敢向您保證，雖然那樣，但不會有任何興趣上的衝突。

　　我隨信附寄上我的履歷表和我作品的樣本。我可以在星期中的任一天與你面談，只是請在兩天前給我通知，好讓我作適當的安排。如果您有任何問題或想與我聯絡，我的地址和電話號碼就寫在履歷表上。

邱　靜　敬上

The Cover Letter

20, Lane 51,
Hsin Sheng S. Rd.,
Sec. 2,
Taipei 10633

May 25, 2008

Mr. Chen
China Newswire Co., Ltd.
12F, 98, Yenping S. Rd.
Taipei

Dear Mr. Chen:

I would like to apply for a job you advertised in the Bulletin Board of the Mandarin Language Training Center of Shur Da. My experience in writing dates back to my college years.

In the ad. you called for someone who can speak and write in Chinese, I am right now studying Mandarin in Taipei. I have been learning the language for a year now. I believe that I am fluent enough in the language to carry out my work in the job satisfactorily.

Enclosed you'll find my resume. Please give me a ring in my apartment at your convenience. I hope to hear from you soon.

Sincerely yours,

Heather Lehr

附函英漢對照

台北市 10633 新生南路
二段 51 巷 20 號

2008 年 5 月 25 日

台北市延平南路
98 號 12 樓
中國新聞網有限公司
陳先生

親愛的陳先生：

　　我想應徵貴公司在師大國語教學中心公布欄上所廣告的工作。我的寫作經驗開始於我大學時代。

　　在廣告中貴公司要求一個能說寫中文的人，我現在就在台北學中文。我已經學這語言學了一年了。相信我對這語言的流利程度可使我執行工作令人滿意。

　　你會看到我附寄的履歷表。請在您方便的時候打電話到我公寓給我，希望很快有您的回音。

希瑟雷爾　敬上

The Cover Letter

3907 Vardell Road N.W.
Calgary, Alberta
Canada

May 10, 2008

General Manager
Asian Lifestyle Magazine
4F 98 Chun Shan South Road,
Taipei, Taiwan, ROC

To whom it may concern:

Please look over my application for a position of staff writer in your magazine. Although my work experience has taken me away from my original vocation in life, writing, I'm sure if you'll look over my record in the university you will appreciate what I have achieved.

I'll be coming over to Taipei in maybe two to three months' time. I'll appreciate it very much if you'll grant me an interview so I can tell you more about myself. In the meantime, if you may, please write to me at my address in Canada.

Enclosed you'll find my resume and a sample of my work. Hoping to hear from you soon.

Faithfully yours,

Peter Oliva

enc.

** vocation〔voˊkeʃən〕*n.* 職業

附函英漢對照

加拿大亞伯達卡加利
瓦得爾西北路 3907 號

2008 年 5 月 10 日

中華民國台灣台北市
中山北路 98 號 4 樓
亞洲生活風貌雜誌
總經理

敬啓者：

　　請看過我的申請後，在貴雜誌安排一個寫作員的職位。雖然我的工作經驗已和我生命中第一個職業，寫作，不相關了，我確定如果您看過我的大學記錄，您會欣賞我做成的事情。

　　我將到台北去，或許就在兩三個月內。如果您能面試我，讓我跟您多談談我自己，將不勝感激。同時，如果您可以的話，請寫信到加拿大的地址給我。

　　您可看到我附寄的履歷表和作品樣本。希望很快有您的回音。

彼得奧利瓦　敬上

有附件

The Cover Letter

P.O. Box 91-124, Taipei, Taiwan R.O.C.
Tel. (02) 702-9119 Telex 24177 FCTRADE,
Att. Martyn Green

19th February 2008

Dear Sirs:

I am writing in reference to your advertisement for an Editor/Writer.

I am enclosing my resume, and I would be grateful if you would seriously consider my application since I believe that I am well qualified for the position, having been a freelance writer/photographer for over seven years, and also having worked as an assistant editor on several magazines. I am now the Editor of an electronics magazine.

As you can see, I obtained a bachelor's degree in California, before going on to study for a graduate degree in Columbia University, New York. Should you be interested, I would consider myself reasonably cognizant with the "Wordstar" word processing programme -- I use it every day in my Epson PX portable computer. (I have even taken this computer to the top of the highest mountain in Southeast Asia, Mt. Kinabalu -- see "China Post" Feb. 14th, last year.)

I think you will agree that I am, at least, a strong candidate for the position you are offering.

** cognizant〔ˈkɑgnɪzənt〕*adj.* 認識的

　portable〔ˈportəbḷ,ˈpɔr-〕*adj.* 手提式的

附函英漢對照

中華民國台灣台北市郵政信箱 91-124

電話（02）702-9119　Telex 24177 FCTRADE，馬丁格林

2008 年 2 月 19 日

敬啓者：

我寫這封信是和你廣告徵求編輯／寫作有關。

附寄上我的履歷表，如果你很認眞地考慮我的申請，我會很感激，因爲我相信我非常有資格作這職務，我曾當過七年以上的自由作家／攝影師，也在很多雜誌社作過助理編輯。現在是一份電子雜誌的編輯。

正如你可見到．在繼續紐約市哥倫比亞大學研究所學位的攻讀之前，我是在加州拿到學士學位的。如果你感興趣的話，我認爲自己對 Wordstar 文字處理程式有合理程度的認識——我每天都使用我艾帕森PX‐8 型手提電腦。（我曾帶著這部電腦到東南亞第一高峯，金乃巴羅頂峯上——見去年 2 月 14 日英文中國郵報。）

我想你會同意至少在你所提供的職位上，我是個有實力的候選者。

Should you wish to have more information, I would be
happy to come and see you at a mutually convenient time.
I should add that if you wish, you may call me any time
after about 10:30 a.m., before February 28th, when I
shall be moving to another residence (telephone number
unknown). However, please make sure that you do get me,
as I cannot be sure my roommate will pass on any message
if I am out. My postal address will remain the same.

Yours faithfully,

Martyn Green

Enc.

【 自我推薦的附函首段 】：

I have been a long time admirer of your company
and have followed the growth of Wang Laboratories since
its inception. The men and women of Wang Lab have a
reputation for dedication, hard work, and intelligence.
I would be proud to join this winning team.

I believe my qualifications will show that my
abilities meet your high standards. But in addition to
my qualifications is my enthusiam for work, I love to
work and don't mind putting in 14 hours a day working
for a company I believe in, such as Wang Laboratories.

如果你想要更多的資料，我很樂意在彼此都方便時去見你。如果你
希望，我會補充的，大約上午十點半後，你可以隨時打電話給我，
在二月二十八日之前，那時我將搬到另一處住所（電話號碼還不知
道）。但是，請確定你聯絡到我了，因為我無法確定如果我外出時，
我室友會替我傳留言。我的郵遞住址仍然照舊。

馬丁格林　敬上

有附件

【**要點提示**】：*未透過報紙或親友介紹時，附函可書寫如下例。*

　　我長久以來就一直是貴公司的景慕者，並從成立時就跟隨王氏研究
室成長。王氏研究室的男男女女都以奉獻、勤奮、聰穎稱譽。加入這支
勝利軍，我會感到很榮幸。

　　我相信我的資格將顯示出我的能力可以符合貴公司的高標準。但是
除了我的資格外，是我對工作的熱誠。我喜歡工作，並且不介意一天投
入十四個小時為我所信任的公司工作，像是王氏研究室。

The Cover Letter

4F, 87 Sungkiang Rd.,
Taipei

July 10, 2008

Mr. Frank Litton
Department of Dance
National Taiwan Academy
of Arts
Taipei

Dear Mr. Litton:

I'm writing in response to a vacancy in your department for a French Language teacher. I have learned of this information from Prof. Shih. I'm quite competent to teach French although my current work involves the teaching of French culture only.

I understand that the person you are looking for should be able to work during the evenings. Presently I'm working only in the mornings on Mondays, Wednesdays and Fridays. I'm relatively free on other days and in the afternoons. Although I may occasionally stay in school in the afternoons on Mondays and Fridays for student consultations. I think I can work in the evenings for you without too much pressure on my side.

I would like to set an appointment with you on any day that is convenient to you and when I am available. You can reach me in my office (Department of French, Chinese Culture University. 871-0390.) or at my home (592-9384). Hoping to hear from you soon. Thank you very much.

Sincerely yours,

Livvy Yu

** competent〔ˈkɑmpətənt〕*adj.* 勝任的；能幹的

consultation〔ˌkɑnsḷˈteʃən〕*n.* 請教；諮詢

附函英漢對照

台北市松江路
87 號 4 樓

2008 年 7 月 10 日

台北市國立藝專
舞蹈科
福蘭克李頓 先生

親愛的李頓先生：

　　我是回覆貴科法文老師缺額一事。這則消息是從許教授處得知的。教法文，我相信能夠勝任，雖然我目前的工作僅僅涉及法國文化的教學。

　　我知道貴科所要找的人必須能在晚間工作。現在我只有星期一、三、五早上工作。在其它的日子和下午我比較地空閒。雖然我可能偶爾星期一和星期五下午留在學校，讓學生問問題。我想我可以在晚間為貴科工作，而在我這方面沒有太大的壓力。

　　我很想跟您訂個會面的時間，在任何一個對您方便對我也可行的日子。您可以和我辦公室聯絡（中國文化大學法文系，871-0390）或者我家（592-9384）。希望很快有您的回音，非常謝謝。

余麗薇　敬上

The Cover Letter

195 Minsheng E. Road,
Taipei 10205

September 23, 2008

Ms. Miles Skeat
Administrative Department
Hua-mei Language Institute,
4th Fl., 78,
Chung Shan N. Rd., Sec. 1,
Taipei

Dear Ms. Skeat:

I have learned from the advertisement in the United Daily News of September 19 that you are looking for someone to fill in your vacancy for an English Instructor. With my past experience in the teaching profession and my educational background in this field, I feel I can be considered for the position.

I am right now doing some research at Taiwan University. My schedule leaves me with a lot of time to do other things. Since I have had some experience in teaching English, I'm sure you'll find I can offer a lot to your organization. In my stay in Japan and Hawaii, I've had the chance to work and study in a intercultural environment, so I'm sure this will help a lot in facilitating my teaching your students.

Enclosed you'll also find my resume. I would be glad to have a meeting with you in order to discuss my prospects. Please call me anytime at your convenience at this number 7623155. If I am not around someone will take any messages you may have. I hope to receive your earliest reply. Thank you.

Sincerely yours,

Mei-yu Chao

** vacancy〔'vekənsɪ〕*n.* 空職；空缺　facilitate〔fə'sɪlə,tet〕*v.* 使容易；使便利

台北市 10205 民生東路
195 號

2008 年 9 月 23 日

台北市中山北路一段
78 號 4 樓
華美語文機構行政部門
邁爾斯史吉女士

親愛的史吉女士：

　　我從 9 月 19 日聯合報的廣告得知，你們正在找一個人補英文老師的缺額。我過去的教學經驗，及在這方面的學歷背景，我覺得我可以在這職位上被考慮。

　　我現在正在台大作某項研究。我的計劃留下很多時間給我做其它的事情。因爲我在教英文方面有經驗，我相信妳會發現我可以對貴機構有很大的貢獻。我在日本和夏威夷停留期間，我有機會在不同的文化環境中工作和學習，所以我確信將幫助我更容易教導妳的學生。

　　妳會看到我附寄的履歷表。我會很高興和妳見面來談談我的希望。妳方便時可隨時打 7623155 給我。如果我不在，有人會替妳留話。我希望有妳最快的答覆。謝謝妳。

　　　　　　　　　　　　　　　　　趙美玉　敬上

The Cover Letter

5F-2, No. 19, Hsin Sheng
S. Rd., Sec. 2,
Taipei 10299
June 12, 2008

Mr. Kevin Kendall
Personnel Manager
Cross-Communications Co.
6th Fl., 47,
Hsinyi Rd., Sec. 3,
Taipei

Dear Mr. Kendall:

Please consider me for the position for research
assistant that you advertised in the China Times News
of June 8.

This job is of particular interest for me because
it's the kind of job that I know I'll enjoy and excell
in. As you can see in my resume I've handled many
responsibilities in the various positions I've held.
I'm sure coupled with my educational background I would
be of tremendous service to your company.

I shall be pleased to provide you with any further
details required. I am free to come for interview at
any time.

Sincerely yours,

Su-ling Teng

** excell〔ɪk'sɛl〕 *v.* 優於他人；勝於他人
tremendous〔trɪ'mɛndəs〕 *adj.* 極大的；巨大的

附函英漢對照

台北市 10299 新生南路
二段 19 號 5 樓之二

2008 年 6 月 12 日

台北市 信義路三段
47 號 6 樓
多傳播公司人事經理
凱文坎道爾先生

親愛的坎道爾先生：

　　貴公司在 6 月 8 日中國時報所刊登研究助理一職請考慮用我。

　　我對這份工作特別的感興趣，因為我知道將會喜歡這一類的工作，並能做得比別人好。正如您可以在我的履歷表中看到，我曾經在我所從事不同的職務上，處理過很多的職責。我確信加上我的學歷背景，我將對貴公司有很大的貢獻。

　　我將很樂意提供貴公司更多需要的資料，也隨時有時間面談。

鄧淑玲　敬上

The
Cover
Letter

3, Hoping E. Road,
Sec. 3,
Taipei 10112

December 5, 2008

Mr. Robert Stein
Director, Personnel Department
Atlantic Taiwan Corporation
5F-1, 3, Lane 79,
Fushing S. Rd., Sec. 1,
Taipei

Dear Mr. Stein:

　　I would like to answer the advertisement you placed
in the United Daily News for an executive Interpreter.
If you will look through my resume I am certain that I
can become a valuable addition to your staff.

　　In my college and my present employment, I have
had the chance to learn a lot of things, not only in
the field of my specialization-language interpretation
but also in business. I enjoy meeting people and working
out solutions to problems.

　　I have heard a lot of things about your company
and I'm sure that I can find a very fulfilling career
there.

　　Please call me at this number at any time of the
day except in the evenings. (3417133) I've enclosed my
resume which provides full information about my background.

　　　　　　　　　　　　　　Sincerely yours,

　　　　　　　　　　　　　　Wen-in Fu

附函英漢對照

台北市 10112 和平東路
3 號

2008 年 12 月 5 日

台北市復興南路一段
79 巷 3 號 5 樓之一
台灣大西洋公司人事部門主任
羅勃史登先生

親愛的史登先生：

　　我想回覆貴公司刊登在聯合報徵求執行翻譯的廣告。如果您看過我的履歷表，我確信我會成為貴公司職員中新增的寶貴的一員。

　　在我大學時和現在的工作上，我一直有機會學很多事情，不只是在我專門語言翻譯的領域，還有商業方面。我喜歡會晤人，以及找出問題的解決方法。

　　我聽過很多關於貴公司的事情，而且我確信我能在那兒找到一份非常能夠發揮的職業。

　　除了晚上之外，請在任何時間用這個電話號碼打電話給我。（3417133）我也附上我的履歷表，能提供有關我背景的完全資料。

傅文英　敬上

The Cover Letter

6F 89 Hsin Sheng
S. Road, Sec. 3,
Taipei 10715

February 14, 2008

Mr. Stanly Cheng,
Personnel Manger
Technocraft Applications, Inc.
189 Chung Shan Rd.,
Taipei

Dear Mr. Cheng:

    I'm submitting my resume for your consideration as the general manager that you advertised for in the papers. I am certain with my education in the States and the valuable experience I have gotten from my previous employments both here and in the States, I can be of great service to your company.

    Upon completion of my masters at the American University, I as able to put all the theories I had learned in school to good use. Besides this, I was able to gain a lot of experience in the actual handling of a business. If you would ask me why I took this course, I can only say that I find nothing so rewarding and challenging as being in business.

    Enclosed is my resume and recommendation letters from my teachers and my former employers. Could we set a date to talk about my chances of joining your company? I would appreciate it if you can give a reply at your soonest.

Sincerely yours,

Jieh-Chyi Lai

** submit 〔 səb'mɪt 〕 *v*. 提出某事物

附函英漢對照

台北市 10715 新生南路
三段 89 號 6 樓

2008 年 2 月 14 日

台北市中山路 189 號
工藝技術應用公司
人事經理　史丹利程先生

親愛的程先生：

　　貴公司刊登在報紙上總經理一職，我提出我的履歷表讓貴公司考慮。我確定以我在美國受的教育，及從這裏和美國兩處先前的工作所獲得的寶貴經驗，將對貴公司貢獻很大。

　　基於我在美國大學完成的碩士學位，我得以把我在學校所學的理論都付諸良好的運用。除此之外，在真正處理貿易時，我能得到很多的經驗。如果您問我為什麼選這個方向，我只能說，沒有什麼會像貿易這樣有報酬和具挑戰性的。

　　附上我的履歷表和我的老師及先前雇主的推薦函。我們能定個日期談談加入貴公司的機會嗎？如蒙儘速給予回音，將不勝感激。

賴介琦　敬上

全國最完整的文法書 ☆☆☆

文　法　寶　典

▶ 劉　毅　編著

　　這是一套想學好英文的人必備的工具書，作者積多年豐富的教學經驗，針對大家所不了解和最容易犯錯的地方，編寫成一套完整的文法書。

　　本書編排方式與衆不同，首先給讀者整體的概念，再詳述文法中的細節部分，內容十分完整。文法說明以圖表爲中心，一目了然，並且務求深入淺出。無論您在考試中或其他書中所遇到的任何不了解的問題，或是您感到最煩惱的文法問題，查閱**文法寶典**均可迎刃而解。例如：哪些副詞可修飾名詞或代名詞？(P.228)；什麼是介副詞？(P.543)；那些名詞可以當副詞用？(P.100)；倒裝句(P.629)、省略句(P.644)等特殊構句，爲什麼倒裝？爲什麼省略？原來的句子是什麼樣子？在**文法寶典**裏都有詳盡的說明。

　　例如，有人學了**觀念錯誤的**「假設法現在式」的公式，

> If ＋現在式動詞……，主詞＋shall（will, may, can）＋原形動詞

只會造：If it rains, I will stay at home.
而不敢造：If you ***are*** right, I ***am*** wrong.
　　　　　If I ***said*** that, I ***was*** mistaken.
　　　　　（If 子句不一定用在假設法，也可表示條件子句的直說法。）

可見如果學文法不求徹底了解，反而成爲學習英文的絆腳石，對於這些易出錯的地方，我們都特別加以說明（詳見 P.356）。

　　文法寶典每册均附有練習，只要讀完本書、做完練習，您必定信心十足，大幅提高對英文的興趣與實力。

◉ 全套五册，售價***900***元。市面不售，請直接向本公司購買。

TOEIC 700分保證班

四大卓越特色：
1. 一次繳費，直到考取700分為止。
2. 學費全國最低，並贈送口說、寫作班。
3. 本班最新研發獨家教材。
4. 一次繳費，所有多益班系皆可上課。

台北課程　　　　　　　　一次報名，班班皆可上!!

班　　級		上課時間	收費標準
TOEIC 聽力閱讀班	A班	每週一晚上7：00~9：00	9,900元 / 一期十八週班 19,800元 / 一年期班
	B班	每週日晚上7：00~9：00	29,700元 / 終生保證班
TOEIC口說班		每週二晚上7：00~9：00	9,900元(報名多益班即贈口說班)
TOEIC寫作班		每週三晚上7：00~9：00	9,900元(報名多益班即贈寫作班)

台中課程　　　　　※ 實際上課時間以本班最新公告為準。

班　　級		上課時間	收費標準
TOEIC 聽力閱讀班	A班	每週六下午2：00~4：00	9,900元 / 一年期班 19,800元 / 終生保證班
	B班	每週四晚上7：00~9：00	
TOEIC口說班		不限次數約定上課	9,900元(報名多益班即贈口說班)

1. 問：什麼是「TOEIC 700分保證班」？

   答：凡是報名保證班的同學，我們保證你考到700分。如果未達700分，就可以免費一直上課，考上700分為止，絕不再另外收費，但是你必須每年至少考一次TOEIC測驗，考不到700分，可憑成績單，繼續上課。

2. 問：如果考到700分，或一年都沒去考試，還可以繼續上課嗎？

   答：(1) 開始上課日一年內，沒有TOEIC測驗成績單，則必須再交9,900元，才可繼續上課；即使沒來上課，你也須參加考試憑成績單保留上課權益。

   (2) 如果TOEIC測驗考到700分以上，可再交9,900元，考到800分為止；如考到800分，想再繼續上課，須再交9,900元，保證考到900分為止。

劉毅英文教育機構

台中總部：台中市三民路三段125號7F（李卓澔數學樓上）　　TEL：（04）2221-8861
台北本部①：台北市重慶南路一段10號7F（火車站前・台企大樓）　TEL：（02）2361-6101
台北本部②：台北市許昌街17號6F（火車站前・壽德大樓）　　　TEL：（02）2389-5212

如何寫好英文履歷表

修　　編／陳　瓊　芳

發　行　所／學習出版有限公司　　　☎ (02) 2704-5525

郵 撥 帳 號／0512727-2 學習出版社帳戶

登　記　證／局版台業 2179 號

印　刷　所／裕強彩色印刷有限公司

台 北 門 市／台北市許昌街 10 號 2 F　☎ (02) 2331-4060・2331-9209

台灣總經銷／紅螞蟻圖書有限公司　　☎ (02) 2795-3656

美國總經銷／Evergreen Book Store　☎ (818) 2813622

本公司網址　www.learnbook.com.tw

電 子 郵 件　learnbook@learnbook.com.tw

售價：新台幣一百五十元正

2009 年 7 月 1 日新修訂

ISBN 978-986-231-029-8